SIX-FIGURE AGENT

SIX-FIGURE AGENT

CelebrityPress®
Lake Mary, Florida

CONTENTS

CHAPTER 1

YES YOU CAN!

BY TRICIA TURNER

Let me start off by saying, if I can do it, so can you.

I quit school when I was 17, I got kicked out of my house at 17, I did not graduate from college, and I started using drugs at the age of 12. I should be homeless, a drug addict, prostitute...but I'm not. Instead, I am a single mother of three awesome kids, a real estate broker, a successful business owner, an author, and someone absolutely committed to making a difference in this world.

Getting to where I am today and where I plan to go has certainly not been easy, but with self-discipline, hard work, determination, and the belief that you can do anything, I firmly believe that anything is possible. Let me share some of my story with you...

After quitting school at 17, I got my GED immediately. I had been working since the age of 15, so having a job was something already ingrained in me. I then went to college for a short bit, before I decided to go to real estate school and get my real estate license. I had worked in the apartment industry prior to doing real estate sales, and even obtained my loan officers license and was a lender from 2004-2010.

I became a mom in 1997 and that is when I would say I really got serious about what I wanted to achieve in my life. I went on to have two other children and my husband and I were well on our way to building an empire and achieving great success, but I was miserable inside and knew that my marriage was not sustainable.

So, in 2008, at the height of the mortgage crisis, I also told my husband I wanted a divorce. That began my years of struggle and what has now come to really define how I have built and continue to build my own empire.

From 2008 through 2010 were very hard years for me. I was a single mother of three, on a commission-based income, with no financial help or support from my ex-husband, in an industry that had crashed. I lived off of credit cards most of 2010, and in fact amassed $100,000 in credit card debt. It was one of the most stressful times of my life. And to make it even worse, my mother passed away from lung cancer at the end of 2010. I was devastated.

It was at that time that I started attending Lakewood Church, starting reading scripture in the mornings, read my first book in its entirety, and put a plan in place to make it happen...to be the best version of myself and to be the best role model for my three children. At the end of 2010, I let my loan officer's license expire and went back into real estate sales at full force. No days off and no excuses. My kids depended on me and I was not going to let them down. And I have not.

I went on to obtain my real estate broker's license, opened our own real estate brokerage, and have continued climbing the success ladder and opening other businesses related to real estate.

I attribute much of my success to the morning routine that I created, and the perfect day that I am always seeking. Both were formed during the darkest times of my life in 2010.

I believe that you must protect your mind, body and soul at all costs. I believe that what you feed your body is directly connected to your mindset and your success. Therefore, if you do not establish a morning routine and stay laser focused on it, you may never achieve all that your heart desires.

You must first establish a start time for your day. Something that is achievable on a consistent basis. For me, that time is 4:00 a.m. Having a set time to begin the day is the ideal way to start aligning your mind, body and soul. Find a time that fits your lifestyle and your family and stick to it. I have always heard that most millionaires are up before the sun (hint, hint).

Getting your mindset established begins when the alarm goes off the first time, not the second, third or fourth time. That means DON'T HIT THE SNOOZE BUTTON. Pretend that does not exist. Most of us use our smartphones as alarm clocks. Because that smartphone is in your hand as soon as you open your eyes and turn off the alarm, many people have the temptation to begin checking their social media feeds or email messages immediately.

When you check social media or messages as the first thing you do, it places you in a reactive mode. This is not helpful for setting the best possible mindset for the day. Your brain is one of the largest organs in your body, therefore you must constantly be aware of what you are allowing into it. I cannot stress strongly enough the negative consequences this can have on your mindset. Stay focused on your schedule and what your next activity should be.

For me, my morning is very structured. When my alarm goes off, I get up, I put on my workout clothes, I grab a water, and I go to my favorite spot to read. I read books that help me with motivation and with advice on living my best life. I read scripture and I listen to bible verses and a devotional. Often times I will journal during this time. This time is typically blocked out for at least 30 minutes, depending on what my calendar calls for that day.

Once my reading is done, I work out for anywhere from 45 minutes to 90 minutes, depending on the day, and then I'm ready to get prepared for work. While putting on my makeup and doing my hair, I continue feeding my mind by listening to podcasts and/or music that inspires me and gets my mind right. Once I have fed my mind, body and soul, it is time to get to work which typically starts between 8:30 – 9:00. I use my google calendar to plan each day and I stick to what is on my schedule each day.

I was taught many years ago that if you can define what a perfect day is to you, your life will be less chaotic when you achieve it. Therefore, I am always seeking that perfect day and trying to stay in sync with my calendar. Being in the real estate world, we tend to get distracted by shiny objects, which can deter us from getting our highest leveraged activities done. So, you must really adhere to your calendar and what you allow yourself to put on it.

I believe that blocking out a minimum of two hours each morning of the workday is critical to increasing your productivity, which will increase your income. I traditionally block out each weekday morning from 9:00 – noon for prospecting calls, whether they are recruiting calls or lead generating calls. On Fridays, they are follow up calls. I teach my agents to think of all Fridays as 'follow up Fridays' and that's what should be focused on each Friday.

I do not believe in checking email prior to starting the prospecting session unless you have at least 30 minutes to handle any email that may potentially become a distraction. Do not allow being reactive to interrupt your routine and your mindset. Set aside certain times in your routine to react to messages and requests, both by text and email, rather than responding to them randomly throughout the day.

When I arrive at the office, prior to starting my prospecting session, I will organize my day even further. I use a small whiteboard that I keep on my desk to write down my top 3–5 things that MUST get done before I leave that day. This helps me stay focused on what moves the needle. Try not to ever add more than 5, and 3 is actually much better. Quality over quantity. When you have too much on your plate, you tend to work in a less productive state.

Because I run a growing real estate company, our sales agents tend to need help quite often and that in itself can be quite a distraction. So, in order to keep those distractions to a minimum and always be available to our agents, we came up with what we call 'gotta minute?' This is a Zoom link that is on every agent's calendar for 1:00 pm Monday through Friday, and they all know that myself and my COO will be available on that link for at least 30 minutes to help them or answer any questions. That concept has been hugely successful with our time management and for working efficiently. I rely on the rest of the afternoon for appointments, coaching calls, etc., whether face to face or via zoom. I meet with clients, other agents and realtor partners, as well as our preferred partners.

Once the workday comes to an end, it is time to take on activities that you want to do. I believe strongly in trying to create a balance in your life and doing things that bring you happiness, inner peace, and fulfillment. Take some time to figure out what that is and then seek to find the time to do those things. When your children are young and you are establishing your family, there is nothing wrong with scheduling around things that are important to them and imperative to your family. Those things matter.

Whatever time you pick to end your day, make this part of your daily routine. Find what works for you and make that a principle. If you do not take some time to do what feeds your soul, this industry can eat you alive and you will ever find true peace. I know that my life could have been a bit simpler had someone handed me a playbook and the knowledge that I have acquired over the years, but that never happened. My success comes from hard work, grit, determination, and getting myself around others that inspire me.

Unfortunately in the real estate industry, there are many that are successful yet have no desire to help others and they keep their "secrets" to themselves. I call that a scarcity mindset, which I do not believe in. I believe in an abundance mindset. Our company mission is to build better lives by building better agents, and that is what we are about. I have a passion for helping others have as much success in this industry as possible, and I believe it is because of all of the struggles that I have been through in my life.

I believe there is strength in numbers and I believe that we are better together. You must have someone in the industry you can talk to, someone you can count on when things are tough. I know how much I struggled and I certainly do not want others to go through some of the difficulties that I have had to go through. I feel as though God allowed me to go through my dark years so that it would make me stronger, so I could bring my solutions to others and help them avoid their own dark years.

For anyone reading this chapter, know that you can do anything you set your mind to. Yes, it may get overwhelming, but if you will establish a regimented morning routine and then adhere to your daily schedule, you will find that the structure will help you remove the chaos from your mind and from your life. This can be applied to any business as well.

One final thing...DON'T QUIT!

About Tricia

Tricia Turner, of the Tricia Turner Group, was born and raised in Houston and has been in real estate for over 20 years. After practicing real estate and lending for many years, Tricia obtained her real estate broker's license and opened her own independent real estate company.

In October 2018, Tricia left her own brokerage and moved her license over to EXP Realty along with several agents from her brokerage and formed a mega team, which has continued to grow and thrive. Their team has a goal of $100 million in sales volume for 2023.

In addition to the real estate company, Tricia also owns her own staging company, Honeybee Homestaging & More, as well as her own event center, HUB510 along with the private bar, Piggy's Place. All businesses are located in the Katy/Fulshear/Richmond area.

Tricia resides in the Katy/Fulshear area where she has been for over 22 years. She has three children who are all involved in the family businesses.

Tricia is very active in Fort Bend County. She is a member of the Fulshear/Katy Chamber of Commerce and the Brazos River Rotary Club. She is also an ambassador for the Child Advocates of Fort Bend and serves on the Texana Advisory Board.

To learn more about Tricia Turner and her vision, go to:

- www.triciaturner.work

CHAPTER 2

HOLD THE PHONE, PLEASE...!

BY WALLY BRESSLER

No, really.

Hold the phone – in your hand – and make calls so you can build a six-figure real estate business!

As much as technology has changed the way real estate is conducted since the Internet was first made available to the public in April of 1995...agents still need to use the phone to build and grow their business.

Yes, some agents are 'killing it' with social media. Sure, other agents are 'crushing it' with referral and repeat business. And yeah, some other agents are 'slaying it' with video content.

These are good things, don't get me wrong. But these agents are the exception and not the rule, as they represent a very small percentage of the 1.61 million realtors walking the earth in the U.S. at the time this chapter is being written.

THE NUMBERS DON'T LIE

Interestingly enough, a quick look at the statistics tells us that real estate consumers actually WANT to talk to someone before and when they are ready to buy a home. In fact, according to cloud-based communications giant, Ring Central, roughly 50% of Millennials, Gen Xers and Baby Boomers want to talk to someone before making a large purchase.

The truth is, it's not real estate consumers that have an issue with the phone...it's real estate agents who do.

According to Dave Kurlan, CEO and Founder of global sales skills assessment stalwart, Objective Management Group: "60% of salespeople have a very strong need to be liked by their prospects and clients. It's okay to want to be liked, but when your need to be liked interferes with your desire and ability to successfully implement the various steps of the sales process... it becomes a huge obstacle to generating consistent profits."

More specifically, the issue of needing to be liked means that 40% of seasoned sales people and 80% of new salespeople suffer from Call Reluctance as reported by B2B lead generation outfit, CINENCE. When you consider it takes roughly 12 to 15 contacts with buyer prospects to sell one home and/or 55 to 60 contacts with seller prospects to sell a home, you can see how problematic having Call Reluctance can be for a salesperson.

CALL RELUCTANCE IS REAL

Call Reluctance is especially troublesome because real estate is a relationship business. And to build a great relationship with someone, you need to talk to them...regularly, which requires that you get on the phone with them in addition to sending text messages, emails and even meeting with them face to face.

Not only that, no matter how great your marketing and social media presence are, at some point you're going to need to get your prospects on the phone to come meet with you – so you can demonstrate to them why you're the agent of choice for their specific real estate needs.

Having been in the real estate industry for roughly 25 years now – coaching, mentoring or training other agents for 22 of those years – I've seen firsthand how avoiding picking up the phone has been a huge obstacle to agents becoming successful. At the same time, I've seen the businesses of those who are willing to make phone calls skyrocket in a matter of years, and continue to grow exponentially over the span of their career.

In fact, I'm comfortable in saying that the fastest way to making six figures in real estate – and then scaling your business from there – rests heavily on your ability to:

1) make initial calls to prospects
2) make follow up calls to prospects who aren't ready to buy or sell when you first speak with them and...
3) maintain relationships with past clients and the people in your sphere of influence for as long as you are practicing real estate

CALL RELUCTANCE AT A GLANCE

If you suffer from 'fear of the phone', then you probably believe that you'll never want to or be able to use the phone to grow your business.

In fact, you may say things to yourself and others like:

> *"I hate the phone."*
> *"I hate when telemarketers or other salespeople call me."*
> *"I don't want to bother people by calling them."*
> *"It's too early to call."*
> *"It's too late to call."*
> *"People just don't want to be called."*

From there, you likely text and email people to death while trying to connect with them on Facebook by sharing the video of the Surfing Squirrel.

If this is your approach, it's going to be virtually impossible to make six figures in real estate. In fact, you very well might not make it. We MUST talk to people and build relationships with them if we're going to build a sustainable, scalable real estate business.

Here's a closer look at what Call Reluctance looks like in salespeople:

- Powerful negative emotions, such as fear, embarrassment, shame, anxiety, guilt, and even panic
- Negative thoughts and anticipation of the worst ("They don't need it" or "They will turn me down")
- The mental block that keeps a rep from taking an action
- Sometimes, salespeople try to deny their own negative emotional responses. In this case, they try to buy time before calling, resorting to frequent procrastination and/or 'over-preparing' for calls
- Fear of getting in front of a camera to record videos for social media or other business efforts
- Fear of calling past clients and/or sphere to ask for referrals
- Fear of recruiting people to your business or downline to grow your organization
- Beating yourself up in an effort to get on the phone to make calls and/or get in front of the camera to record videos

As you read this list, which one – or how many – of these symptoms affect you when it's time to pick up the phone and prospect and/or nurture leads. In general, Call Reluctance shows up as procrastination, perfectionism, imposter syndrome, self-sabotage and other avoidance strategies.

What's interesting here is that agents with Call Reluctance fall into three categories:

1. They're okay calling people they don't know but would rather die than talk to someone they do know.
2. They're okay calling people they do know but would do anything to not talk to people they don't know.
3. They don't want to talk to people they do know or don't know.

Which category do you fall into when it comes to prospecting?

All of this talk about prospecting and talking to people may be triggering some anxiety and fear in you right now, causing you to have a dry mouth and sweaty palms. It may even be making you lightheaded and giving you an upset stomach. Or, you may have gone completely blank and you've checked out altogether. No matter how you're feeling, if you're experiencing any feelings like these…you likely have some form of Call Reluctance. It's important to understand that having Call Reluctance is not your fault.

What's even more important is that Call Reluctance is not terminal, and you can resolve the issue in way less time than you might think would be possible. That said, it won't go away without you doing the work. I know this because I suffered from Call Reluctance for 10 years before I did what I needed to do in order to make it go away for good.

AWARENESS IS YOUR BEST FRIEND

After conducting more than 40,000 one-on-one coaching calls, live training sessions and group coaching sessions – as well as making more than 75,000 prospecting and follow up calls as a salesperson, business owner and coach – I've determined that in order to overcome Call Reluctance, you must find the root cause and work from there.

To help you narrow down the actual source(s) of your Call Reluctance, I can tell you that it's caused by something that happened between the time you were born and the age of 12 (or 13 the latest). The main source usually comes from one of these categories:

- **Physical, Emotional and/or Sexual Abuse:** Experiencing abuse at any age can have a huge impact on our self-esteem and self-worth. The amount of uncertainty and fear that gets triggered in us from being abused at a young age – whether it was one time or a number of times – can be huge.

- **Bullying:** When we are young, we look for approval and acceptance from our family at home and the people with whom we go to school. These are the two places we spend most of our time and the groups of people we interact with on a regular basis. When we're bullied, ridiculed, made fun of or even made to feel different from others, our need for approval and acceptance takes root and grows like a weed over our lifetime.

- **Hidden Identities:** Sometimes, we form belief systems about what we think we can and can't do, that we're completely unaware of, simply by making observations and comparing ourselves to others—without any inside input. For example, many people who grow up poor have a hidden identity that they are not as good as other people, which negatively impacts their self-worth.

- **Learned belief systems:** For the most part, our parents are the biggest influences in our lives when we are young. What they say and do to us and for us has the biggest impact on what we believe we can and can't do and/or should and shouldn't do. If our parents fought all the time in front of us, then we can easily learn to avoid any situation that could be considered confrontational. Oddly enough, the same thing could happen to us if our parents never fought in front of us when we were children.

It can be one of these experiences or a combination of more than one of them that created the Call Reluctance within us. Essentially, the negative experience triggered our Fight or Flight instinct and our response to what happened was Flight— to run away from the fear and pain so as to avoid it. And if the experience happened more than once, we kept running for the rest of our lives and conditioned our subconscious to avoid things that triggered our Flight response, which can, and usually does, include picking up the phone to call people.

While you've been reading this, your brain has been going back and looking for any and all experiences in your life that could have created Call Reluctance. You see, our brains remember everything we've ever tasted, touched, seen, heard and smelled. So anything negative that occurred in one of the areas I listed above has been logged by your memory and is accessible when you look for it.

In an effort to get super clear on what the true causes are of your Call Reluctance, you can do the following exercise: grab two note cards and on each one of them write down the following question: "What is the source of my Call Reluctance?" If you want to, you can add questions like: "What is the source of my procrastination?" or "What is the source of my perfectionism?" and/or "What is the source of my imposter syndrome?"

Once you've done that, keep one card with you during the day and read it from time to time. Take the other card and put it on your nightstand to read a few times before bed. By the time you wake up the next morning, You should have a very clear picture of the cause(s) of your Call Reluctance.

NOW WHAT?

Canadian Personal Development and Wealth Creation expert, T. Harv Ecker, coined the acronym TFAR, which stands for Thoughts Lead To Feelings Lead To Actions Lead To Results.

The key component in TFAR for folks that have Call Reluctance is the F, which stands for feelings. When it comes time to pick up the phone and start prospecting, negative thoughts get triggered that create fear and anxiety. Instead of letting these negative feelings come up and processing them, we let them create avoidance strategies in us like procrastination and perfectionism.

And it's at this instant that pile of clean laundry on the couch or the dirty dishes in the sink take an inordinate amount of importance in our life and must be dealt with immediately. Oddly enough, if we would just let those feelings come up and pass, we would be able to then pick up the phone and make calls. The great news is that any one of us can let those feelings come up and then let them out the front door of our mind and into the ether through a very simple strategy called mindfulness.

The American Psychological Association defines mindfulness as "...[the] awareness of one's internal states and surroundings." Mindfulness can help people avoid destructive or automatic habits and responses by learning to observe their thoughts, emotions, and other present-moment experiences without judging or reacting to them. By focusing on the present moment – the here and now – we can let those nasty, disempowering emotions bubble up and make their way out, which is all they want to do anyway.

Not surprisingly, avoiding these emotions and pushing them down with drugs, alcohol, cigarette smoking, eating and other avoidance strategies like procrastination and perfectionism is what allows that Call Reluctance to take root and wreak havoc on our business efforts and results. When you complete the notecard exercise as described, you will likely start experiencing some, or all, of the emotions that have been causing your Call Reluctance. They've always been there, but now that you know where they're coming from, you can acknowledge and deal with them.

Here's how to deal with them: the next time you feel uneasy, uncomfortable, anxious, scared, etc. when you need to pick up the phone to prospect or make a call you're not looking forward to, follow this simple three step process:

1. Become aware: Acknowledge your feelings and let them show up. Be aware that they are there and don't rush to avoid them or push them down.
2. Define and identify: These emotions have nothing to do with the phone and making a call. They are just a conditioned response to things that scare or worry you. Knowing this, define what the feelings are and identify where they are coming from, i.e., you were bullied in elementary school, which created a strong need for approval inside you and the desire to avoid any situation – including a prospecting call – where you could be rejected.
3. Become mindful: Wherever you are, stop what you're doing, close your eyes and engage in some square or box breathing: breathe in for a four count, hold for a four count, breathe out for a four count, and hold for a four count. Continue to do this until you're able to regulate your emotions. It takes some practice, but if you do it regularly enough, you'll get control of your emotions and be able to pick up the phone and make calls.

THE GOOD, THE BETTER AND THE BEST

Call Reluctance is not our fault. Our fight or flight response kicked in due to some scary experiences when we were very young. As we grew older, we continued to condition ourselves to avoid things that were scary, and that drummed up fear and anxiety in us...especially as it related to being approved of and accepted by others.

The good news is that we are not stuck with our Call Reluctance. There's something we can do about it to free ourselves from the shackles of inconsistency and self-sabotage. What's even better is that working on the root cause(s) of our Call Reluctance will not only make our businesses more profitable and successful, but it will also help us become happier, more relaxed and significantly less stressed and concerned about what others think about us. The emotional freedom we experience is worth all the effort in working through the issues that cause Call Reluctance.

As I mentioned at the beginning of this chapter, the phone is not going away anytime soon as a means of building business in the real estate industry. More importantly, if you want to make six figures year-in and year-out as a real estate agent, you're going to need to master using the phone to prospect for and nurture sales leads. So, if you do have Call Reluctance of any kind, the best thing you can do for yourself, your family and your business is to locate the root cause of the problem and then work on processing the negative emotions that arise when it's time to pick up the phone and call.

When you do this work, there is no limit to the amount of money you can make in real estate and to the things you can accomplish in life.

About Wally

Wally Bressler's goal in life is to help people realize that they don't need to hit rock bottom in order to make the changes necessary to enjoy a joyful and fulfilling life.

Wally has conducted over 40,000 coaching sessions via one-on-one calls, live training sessions, group calls, and video-training meetings with real estate sales professionals across the United States and Canada. He's had the good fortune of working with some of the top real estate agents and coaches in North America...where he's learned as much from them as they did from him.

In 2021, as a result of his efforts in helping his clients achieve great success in their businesses and lives, he was nominated for *Success* magazine's Success 125 – one of the 125 Most Influential People in Real Estate That Get Results.

In addition to having 22 years of coaching experience, he also has 25 years of sales and real estate experience, as well as 29 years of professional writing experience. He was the ghost writer on two Amazon published books, *Inside Sales Predictability* and *Digital President* and released his own book, *Tragic Hero: Picking Up The Pieces*, in early September of 2022, which became an Amazon Best Seller. In it, he uses the lessons he's learned from overcoming lifelong addictions to food, sex, pornography, and money to give others the hope and confidence they need to overcome their own challenges. The book attained bestseller status in four separate categories on Amazon.

In November of 2022, Bressler was a guest on *Times Square Today*, which airs on ABC, NBC, CBS, and FOX. On the show, he shares some of the strategies he uses to help entrepreneurs and salespeople create amazing businesses and lives by overcoming self-sabotage, low self-esteem, procrastination and perfectionism.

Prior to his coaching career, Wally started as a real estate agent in 1998, selling 72 homes during his first 14 months in the business. As he grew with the company where he started his sales career, he became a sales manager and trainer, and helped grow the team to more than 400 home sales annually.

Wally graduated from Hamilton College in 1990 and started his working career in the mutual fund industry in 1991, where he worked for seven years before he made the leap to the real estate industry.

In 2021, Wally started Phone Sales Secrets (now Trigger Sales System), a company that helps salespeople overcome sales Call Reluctance, procrastination, self-sabotage, procrastination, and other avoidance behaviors so that they can become fearless and confident in using their phone sales skills to grow their business. The process he uses comes from what he's learned as a coach as well as from his own experience in dealing with sales Call Reluctance for a decade.

Wally currently lives in McKinney, TX and has four amazing children. He is a regular member and volunteer at Crosspoint Church in McKinney and engages in other community-service-related activities in and around where he lives.

Connect with Wally:

- wally@triggersalessystem.com
- Facebook, Instagram, Twitter, LinkedIn: @wallybressler
- www.triggersalessystem.com

CHAPTER 3

'THE MILLION DOLLAR FOLLOW UP SYSTEM'

BY ALBIE STASEK

I believe that collectively, real estate agents leave millions of dollars in commissions on the table every year, because they were never taught an effective follow up system to convert their buyer and seller leads to sales. If you followed a proven, repeatable, follow up system that is easy to implement and commit to, how many more sales would you have closed in the last twelve months? I encourage you to take five minutes and do the math. How much income fell through the cracks?

I know when I asked myself this question, the ugly truth was a big number. It was a number that made me a little sick. If I'm being 100% transparent, conservatively I lost $200,000 to $400,000 per year. I don't know about you, but I can do a lot with that kind of extra income. You can invest in your family's future. You can give more to your favorite charities. You can invest it back into your business, or... you can blow it on yourself. Whatever you'd do with it, I think we can all agree that it's too much to lose.

Because of this belief, I collaborated with Coach Michael Burt and my business partner, Jay Kinder, to write a book, *Million*

Dollar Follow Up for Real Estate Agents. At the end of this chapter, I will give you information on the book and a 4-hour Master Class on this follow up system. I'm going to share with you one powerful strategy from our book that you can implement and deploy into your business today that costs you nothing but will have a powerful effect on your follow up and lead conversions.

About 73% of real estate prospects work with the first real estate agent that connects with, and then meets with them. The problem is that 80% of prospects take 7-14 touches to convert a lead to an appointment. Most agents aren't pushing past call #1 or #2, not because they are lazy (okay, sometimes we are lazy) but because they were never taught how to follow up like a pro.

Let's study some quick facts and statistics:

- 95% of text messages are read and responded to in three minutes.
- A short, personalized video text will be opened 25% more often than just text alone.
- 85% of consumers want to work with agents who utilize video.

Because of these facts, we found that a personalized video text message is one of, if not the most effective strategy, for getting connected with and converting buyer and seller real estate leads.

It's true. The power of a 30-second video of you talking directly to your prospects and clients via video text is unmatched by virtually any other medium – email, social media or direct mail video – to get and hold their attention.

Important to note. Sending a video text message does not replace the need to actually have a real conversation with your prospects. But this strategy is the best proactive way to connect fast with your prospects, and dramatically increase your conversion rates from lead to client.

VIDEO IS JUST BETTER. PERIOD.

Here's a closer look as to why video works so well and how it can be a game changer for you in your real estate business.

Here's a shocking statistic that most people don't know:

According to a recent finding by Diode Digital...video, as a marketing tool, is 600% more effective than print and mail combined.

Here's why:

- **It's more personal:** Sure, getting text messages, emails, direct messages, and even snail mail, is nice. But it's so much more personal and impactful when there's a video included. Consider the onslaught of well wishes people get on Facebook when it's their birthday. While most folks post a nice sentence or two, or a meme, there are a few people who record customized birthday wishes. You've likely gotten one and it absolutely stood out from the crowd, making you feel even more special than you already did. That's how your prospects and clients feel when you send them a personalized video.

- **It shows you care:** There's some real wisdom in the saying: "It's the thought that counts." We've all swung and missed and given a gift that wasn't a homerun to the receiver. It happens. And most folks, when they receive a gift that missed the mark, will say "Thank you, it's the thought that counts."

  The same can be said for a video text. Rather than simply sending a text or an email, you've taken the time to show you care by putting in that extra effort for your prospect. They, too, will be impressed because you took the time to create a video just for them.

- **It's a stronger way to convey emotion:** Yes, you can paint an amazing picture with words; no doubt. But nothing conveys emotions more effectively than a video where the viewer can hear the words and see the body language of the person on the screen. Rapport is most easily built through physiology, which allows you, the video maker, to connect with your audience faster and easier through video.

More importantly, you can transfer sincerity, authenticity, empathy, excitement and so many other emotions so much more effectively with a video, where people can see your face and hear your tone of voice.

Remember, people buy with emotion and justify with logic. Simply sending a text with details about a home or a great buying opportunity doesn't even scratch the surface of establishing an emotional connection the way video does.

And then there's this...

Robert Cialdini, in his best-selling book, *Influence, the Psychology of Persuasion*, details six main principles of influence: Reciprocity, Commitment, Social proof, Authority, Liking, and Scarcity.

While all of these principles can be leveraged in a video text, there are two of them that you can employ extremely effectively with a personalized video:

1. **Reciprocity:** The Principle of Reciprocity states that people feel the need to reciprocate kindness and thoughtfulness to those who extend them the same courtesy. Earlier, we identified how a personalized video can have such a positive impact on your prospects and clients that they feel special for having received a video from you.

   Through the Principle of Reciprocity, your prospects and clients are more likely to respond to you – and even choose to work with you – because you've sent a video (or videos) to them that makes them feel valued and special. Additionally, if you're delivering specific value that can make the home-selling and/or home-buying process more financially advantageous, helpful, and exciting, the level of reciprocity you receive from the people who get your videos will be even higher.

2. **Like/Liking:** The Principle of Like/Liking states that people want to do business with those that they like or that they think are like them. When you send a personalized video via text to a prospect, they'll see your surroundings, see your face, hear your voice, and get a look at how you're dressed. The combination of these elements allows the viewer to get a more complete picture of who you are and what you're about.

The more details they can collect from your video, the easier it will be for them to determine whether they like you – or that they are like you. More importantly, they'll be able to make the decision that they like – or do not like you – quickly, which means you can make progress more quickly with the folks that like you.

IMPLEMENTING A VIDEO TEXTING STRATEGY

As with most technology offerings in the real estate industry, there are lots of squirrels to chase and shiny things to distract you from what's important: creating and sending 30-second videos.

To help you whittle down your options and get to making and sending videos faster, we're sharing our two favorite video creation and delivery tools here:

I. Reach (www.reachtheapp.com)

Reach is an easy-to-use app available for iPhone and Android phones. With Reach, it's literally as easy as one, two, three:

1. Record your video and be sure to keep it around 30 seconds for easy texting and for consumption by your prospect.

2. Write the message that you're sending along with the video. You should tell your recipient that you recorded a video just for them in your message.

3. Tap on your recipient's name, attach the video, and send.

II. Bomb (www.bombbomb.com)

If you're inclined to use email, as well, you'll want to check out Bomb Bomb. Bomb Bomb is the gold standard of video delivery via email and it's used by real estate agents across the US and Canada.

SAY WHAT?

While there is no one-size-fits-all video that you can send out to everyone, there are a few guidelines you should follow to ensure you make a great video:

1. **Be in a well-lit area.** You can be in a car, on the beach, in a restaurant or anywhere else you want to be… just make sure the area around you is well lit so your viewer can see you and your surroundings. As well, be sure that the light source isn't directly in your eyes or directly behind you. Both of those directions will impact how you look to your viewers.

2. **Make sure you can be heard.** Your message could be the most impactful, amazing message you've ever delivered. It won't matter if your prospect or client can't hear you. Now, you may be wanting to add some excitement to your video by being at an event or in a crowd of people. If you do that, be sure that you have a microphone that picks up your voice and limits the background noise so you can still be heard.

3. **Use their first name.** We never address friends with Mr. or Mrs. and rarely do we use their first and last name when sending them a message. Using the prospect's first name lets them know immediately that you cared to take the time to personally recognize them not as a "lead", but as a human

being. And, that you are also a human, not just some bot or auto-reply message triggered by their inquiry.

4. **Keep it short and sweet.** This is not the time to shoot a 2-3 minute video with your bio and accolades. In 30-40 seconds, your video – if done right – can connect, build trust and authority, and demonstrate you are an agent who plays the game like a professional.

5. **Not too slow, not too fast...just right.** Pace is something that you will master the more you shoot and send these videos. Relax and speak to the prospect like you would if they were right in front of you. If you go too fast, they may not understand you. If you go too slow, they may lose interest. Oh, and don't forget to smile. :)

SAMPLE VIDEOS SCRIPTS

Here are some video scripts that you can R&D (rip off and deploy) for use in your own video creation strategies:

New Buyer Lead

Hi [Use their name], this is [Your name] with [Your company]. Thanks for going to my site to look at homes. I'm reaching out to let you know that I saw your request for more information on [property address or addresses]. I specialize in [their search area] and I'd love to learn more about what you're looking for in a home. Let's find some time to set up a customized search of homes for you and then go out to see some homes. Text me back and let me know when a good time would be for us to connect. Thanks again for reaching out.

Expired Seller Lead

Hi [Use their name], this is [Your name] with [Your company]. By now you know your home at [their address] has come off the market and you're likely not happy about it. I'm sorry that's happened for you. I specialize in selling homes that didn't sell the first time they were listed and I'd love to share with you why your home didn't sell. I'd love to talk with you about what you need to do to get your home sold this time. Text me back and let me know when a good time would be for us to connect so I can show you how to get your home sold. Thanks in advance.

FSBO

Hi [Use their name], this is [Your name] with [Your company]. I'm reaching out about your home at [their address]. I'm currently working with a number of buyers that I'd like to make available your house for their consideration. When would be a good time for me to come by and take a look at your home to see if it matches any of their criteria? My goal is to come over and not take a lot of your time while I'm there. Text me back and let me know when a good time would be for me to come by and take a look at your home. Thanks in advance.

Follow up

Hi [Use their name], this is [Your name] with [Your company]. I was checking in to see how your home search was coming along. We spoke a while back about your home search here in [City Name] and you mentioned that you were going to be looking more seriously starting now. When would be a good time for us to get on the phone to set up a customized search of homes for you and get you out to see some of them? Text me back and let me know when a good time would be for us to connect.

Past Client/Sphere

Hi [Use their name], this is [Your name]. Just wanted to send a quick video to let you know that you were on my mind. Please remember that I'm here for you if you need anything. Let me know if there's anything that I can do for you or your family.

Would love to catch up over the phone or in person. Let me know when a good time to connect would be.

ACTION STRATEGY

These scripts are just recommendations to help get you started. You can use as much or as little of them as you want. The most important thing is that whatever you choose to say...take action. The sooner you put this strategy to work, the sooner you can start building and strengthening relationships with anyone.

See you at the top or from the top!

Get your copy of *Million Dollar Follow Up for Real Estate Agents*

Get the complete strategy! Get your copy of our book *Million Dollar Follow Up for Real Estate Agents* with our 'paint by numbers', easy to deploy system. Go to: FollowUpToMillions.com.

<u>Bonus:</u> The first 100 agents to get the book will also get a video copy of our 4-hour Master Class on Million Dollar Follow Up taught personally by Coach Michael Burt, Jay Kinder and yours truly.

About Albie

Best-selling author, National Speaker, Coach and Icon Award-winning Realtor, Albie Stasek, helps real estate agents, team leaders and brokers scale and grow their business using the most modern digital strategies.

Recognized as a leading expert on marketing, lead generation and video, Albie speaks to audiences internationally on the topics of mindset, team building and content creation.

As an entrepreneur, concert promoter, founder and owner of multiple businesses, Albie oversees a portfolio of companies including: Co-founder of Honey Badger Nation of eXp Realty (HBN is a community of over 13,000 real estate agents, team leaders and brokers in the US, Canada and 10 other Countries who closed over 30,000 transactions in 2022), Icon Cowork – a co-working environment designed for entrepreneurs and business owners to collaborate and grow their businesses more profitably and invest in multi-family real estate holdings.

Albie founded Rock N Rescue CLE, a concert in his hometown of Cleveland Ohio that raises money for charities that rescue women and children from human trafficking. He has been seen in *USA Today, The Plain Dealer,* and has appeared on *New Day Cleveland,* ABC, NBC, CBS, and FOX television affiliates across the country.

Albie is a member of the Ohio and National Association of Realtors. In 2022, he was a recipient of the Social Justice Impact Award for his work and contributions to fight human trafficking in Ohio as well as globally.

Albie also enjoys playing Hockey, Tennis, Golf, Snowboarding, Scuba Diving and rooting for THE Ohio State University Buckeyes with his two children, Aiden and Matthew…and their dog Snoop Dogg.

Learn more at:

- www.Iconcowork.com
- www.AlStasek.com
- www.HoneyBadgerNation.com
- www.FollowUpToMillions.com

CHAPTER 4

THE ChampionSHIFT

BY BOBBY DAVIDOWITZ

It was June of 2006 and I was off on my first trip to Europe. I was headed to Europe with one of my best friends and my business partner. I was 27 and feeling on top of the world. My real estate career up to this point was short but eventful.

At 22, I began my journey in the mortgage business. I got into the real estate world by accident. I was working at a Downtown Orlando night club which was interesting, considering a year before I had graduated with honors from the University of Florida. I had made the mistake of focusing simply on being good at school and making people proud. I had never really sat down and asked that scary question; what the F&%$ did I want to do with my life? For the first time in my life, I felt completely lost. I knew I wanted to do big things in the world and I wanted to be wealthy, but had no idea how I was going to get there. So until I figured things out, I was in a holding pattern shucking liquor bottles and trash cans as a barback.

In a chance meeting at the gym, I met a gentleman who was opening a branch of a mortgage company. Worn down by the late nights at the club and the feeling I wasn't living up to my potential, I was open to opportunity. Two months prior I had drawn a line in the sand. I told myself that by my birthday I was going to leave the club, new job opportunity or not. It was birthday month. Feeling like this was a sign, when that gentleman asked if I would like to try my hand at the mortgage game, I said yes.

Those who are in real estate know that in the beginning the learning curve is steep, and you're drinking through a firehose. It's trial by fire. Those who make it through the fire have the chance of being great if they respect the opportunity and decide to become true professionals. Those who don't make it through the fire are out of the game. It's that famous real estate saying, "you don't get fired in real estate, you fire yourself." It was no different for me. I thought about giving up several times in the first six months but I decided to keep fighting. Watching your bank account drop before your eyes is not for the faint of heart, but for those who fight through, it makes you stronger. Around month five, the bank account was at critical levels and sure enough a few loans came through. I like to say, "God's timing has a frustrating perfection." It never happens as fast as you want, but it's always right on time.

Seeing my bank account go back to previous levels gave me some much needed confidence. Around this time another chance meeting occurred. I met an older gentlemen who worked for another mortgage company. His name was David Levine. David saw something in me. From the first time I met him I could tell he was a good man, and he asked me if I was open to a new mortgage opportunity. Tony Robbins says that growth equals happiness. He's right, I'm only happy when I'm growing and 6 months into the business I was already feeling like I needed to go to a new level that didn't exist where I was. David suggested I meet the president of his company, so I did. Richard was a tall, husky, Missouri country boy turned mortgage professional. He was well dressed in a smooth business casual way that came off cool. He was 31 but looked a bit older and he was skeptical of hiring a relatively inexperienced loan officer. He said he would hire me on if David mentored me. David accepted, and I was off to my next adventure in the mortgage business.

I don't talk about David often, but he was pivotal. He was a man who had some rough patches in life but fought through. He was smart and respected. I'll never forget he had a picture with President Clinton in his office. His latest rough patch was nothing of his doing. He had fought cancer off a few years back, but soon after I started, the cancer came back with a vengeance. Things changed quickly. It went from me driving us to appointments to me driving him to the hospital. David taught me so much. I could tell that he really enjoyed watching me grow, but he also got a kick out of watching a young man getting into young man 'shit'. I think it reminded him of the old days. Needless to say, we both enjoyed our time together. Three months later, I was speaking at David's funeral.

After David's passing, things began moving in warp speed. With David's guidance, I became a top producer within 12 months. Shortly after, Richard, who was not getting along with the owner of the company, asked me if I wanted to start a new mortgage company. What I didn't know about business I compensated for in pure young man over-confidence. So of course I agreed, and we were off. At the time of the 2006 Europe Trip, we were three years into our mortgage company. We had several rough patches at the beginning, but we were doing well. I only mention the Europe Trip because it captured the sentiment of 2006. We spent 16 days in multiple countries—drinking, smoking, eating, and partying. We even have a picture of us riding camels in Morocco! Real estate prices were going up and it seemed they would never go down. Interest rates were at all-time lows. And everyone was crushing it in real estate. Sound familiar?

We know what happened next. Picture a dumpster fire, but worse. The whole financial world went up in flames, including mine. A few years later I would end up losing my house, my car, and filing bankruptcy. This might sound like a sad story but I assure you it is one of great opportunity, and for those who read this chapter, it can be the most prosperous season of your real estate career.

I'm 43 at the time I'm writing this chapter, and what I'm about to reveal to you is the coaching I would have given my 27-year-old self. It's like I'm coming to you from the future to give you all the chess moves in advance. My name is Bobby Davidowitz, but I go by Coach Bobby Franchise. I develop 'Franchise Players' in the real estate game. In 2015, I came back into the real estate business on the Realtor side. The quick story feels like *deja vu*. I quickly became a top producer. I partnered with the broker of the company. And currently, we have 1300 agents in 18 plus states and multiple countries in the EXP Realty model. In addition to building the company, I have been coaching real estate agents, team leaders, and brokers for the past 5 years.

See, when the market crashed in 2007-2008, not everyone crashed. Some people won, and they won big. If you're in real estate, I am telling you, this is the best time to be in real estate and stay in real estate. That doesn't mean everyone will win. It means those with the right mindset, and the actions to match, will win. My coaching brand is structured from my real estate experience and my experience playing football for 9 years of my life. I learned early on that sports mimic life. What it takes to succeed in sports is what it takes to succeed in life. Everything is a game, and real estate is no different. I have a mantra in my coaching program: 'The 4th Quarter is NOW.' Put simply, it means that you never know when your clock is up, so you must live and act as if the 4th quarter is NOW. When things get hard in real estate some run and some become champions. Ladies and Gentlemen, this is The ChampionSHIFT.

Below are the top three plays to win The ChampionSHIFT and create wealth in real estate during a season that today's average realtor has never seen – a down market.

Play 1: Watch your blindside – When a quarterback drops back to pass the ball he often turns his body in a certain direction to throw the ball. The side his back faces is called the blindside because he can't see the defenders coming to crush him from that side. Regardless of whether he can see the defender, the quarterback MUST acknowledge the fact that a monster is coming to get him. When a quarterback stands still, doesn't take action, and lingers too long in the same spot, SMACK!

Pretending that markets don't operate in cycles is the same exact thing, SMACK! When I was 27, I had only really seen up markets. Like many of the investors at the time, I turned a blind eye to the monster that was coming. The reality is, that you can turn that monster into your best friend if you know it's coming. Down cycles are not only coming, but they are also necessary. It is not logical, or good, for prices to keep rising indefinitely. You can't 'buy low' and 'sell high' if there are no lows. *Volatility is where wealth is built.* If you anticipate the monster, you can put yourself in position to score.

I got hit in my first cycle experience. I'm blessed that I did. This time I know exactly what's coming and how to capitalize. Read on.

Play 2: Run towards daylight – When you see a football play drawn on a black board, it is a very organized set of X's and O's, and a series of arrows outlining exactly how things should play out. 'Shit ain't like that' and 'Life ain't like that.'

When a running back gets the ball in the backfield, it doesn't matter what was drawn on that board, it is chaos. Once in a while, the play works perfectly. Most of the time where the opportunity was supposed to be is not where it is. That door closes. The best running backs are the ones who are the best at identifying the new opportunity when things begin to SHIFT. When bodies shift new openings happen, and a great running back RUNS TOWARDS DAYLIGHT.

If you're in real estate, here is your daylight: your competition is leaving the industry and every segment of the market is full of money-making opportunities. I've been teaching a seminar recently called, *Investor Season*. The premise being that this is the cycle when investors flood the market. You want to make money? Learn to work with investors, market to investors, and become an investor. You'll not only have more business, but remember that investors are repeat customers, they buy more than once! But don't stop there. Stack cash and invest in properties yourself!

But here's the deal, it's not just Investor Season. It's buyer season, seller season, builder season, hell, it's even commercial season. Buyers finally have some power again and you need to get them ready to buy. Time to get your buyers lower prices, closing cost assistance, and even get the seller to buy their interest rate down!

Sellers need you more than ever! You can't just slap a property up and get 20 offers. Sorry. You can't go 'For Sale By Owner' and get a cash offer at your door. Nope. Sellers need an agent who knows how to prepare the home for maximum profit, price the property for maximum competition, market the property like a pro, and negotiate like a boss. Go make that listing money!

Remember when builders got cocky? SOME builders, and I won't mention any names, decided you were expendable and drastically lowered their commissions. Oh, how times have changed. I'm getting calls and emails rolling out red carpets and speaking of additional commissions and bonuses. Builder cancellations are up, and buyers are down. If you're in an area where new construction is prevalent, you can make this your niche and clean up!

My point is this: Be a great running back, look for the openings, and *RUN TOWARDS DAYLIGHT!*

Play 3: Go Pro – I don't want to sound like Liam Neeson here, but to dominate this market "you need a special set of skills." You need to make a decision. When I talk to an agent I can always tell when they haven't made THE decision. It's the decision to become a true professional at their craft. It's the decision to GO PRO.

Real estate is not a game for dabblers. To become a champion you have to commit to two things. You have to commit to putting in the time and you have to commit to being a student of the game. Your competition is leaving the industry, but since you're staying, get ready to work. Stop part timing the business and go pro. Immerse yourself in the game. Learn the game. Learn about financing and all the new products that exist. Learn how to analyze investments. Learn the formulas. Learn the programs. Learn the angles of the real estate game. Those who know the most are the most creative, and can get deals done that others can't. A skilled agent will dominate this market! **GO PRO!**

I have now told you the top three winning plays to dominate The ChampionSHIFT. However, there's something I haven't told you. Those plays will never work if you don't believe one thing. It took me years of going to Tony Robbins events and many years of coaching new agents to realize this. I used to think agents were lazy. They would come into my office, desperate, asking me for the million dollar playbook of real estate. I would get their story and I would prescribe them a winning strategy. Three weeks later they would come back, more desperate than before, talking of leaving the business and saying nothing is working. When I would ask if they did what I prescribed, guess what, they would admit they had done nothing.

Here's the deal, you can't win the ChampionSHIFT if you don't believe you deserve it. *Lack of self-worth is the number one killer of dreams.* It's the 'shitty' story you developed in childhood that convinced you that you weren't enough. It's a 'bullshit' story, and you have to kill that monster! I can't tell you exactly how to do it, but it usually starts with you forgiving someone, and it ends with you creating an empowering story about who you are and what you're capable of. I believe you can use real estate as a tool to become the person you desire to be. It is my hope that you do.

About Bobby

Meet Bobby 'Franchise' Davidowitz, the real estate entrepreneur who's committed to using the real estate industry as a wealth creation tool. With over 21 years of experience in the industry, Bobby has had a successful career in lending, investing, and residential and commercial sales.

However, it was four years ago when he combined his expertise in building real estate cultures with the scalable EXP Realty model that he truly started to shine. Through his foundation of coaching and personal development, Bobby has grown his organization to over 1300 agents in 18 states, as well as internationally. His focus on financial freedom drives his mission to partner with agents, brokers, and team leaders to help them create the wealth they desire.

It's no surprise that Bobby recently won the Orlando Real Producers Magazine's "Ultimate Connector" Award for his passion for building relationships with great people in the industry and providing value.

Bobby's drive to help others achieve financial freedom is further exemplified by his love for public speaking. As a national speaker, he delivers energetic speeches on real estate, mindset, and financial freedom.

CHAPTER 5

HOW TO GO FROM GOOD TO GREAT IN REAL ESTATE

BY NICK GOOD

Every kid starts life out with dreams. They dream of what they want to be when they grow up. They dream of how they want their life to go. Whether those dreams are expressed verbally or simply held in the heart, they are there, and many, if not all those dreams want to come to life. Making lots of money very often tops people's dream lists. We want the good things in life. We want to provide for ourselves, and our families. We want to feel confident and secure in being able to enjoy the best that life has to offer. I'm no different. As a kid, I always dreamed of making millions of dollars, and as a teenager, my specific idea of real wealth was having private jet money. So, I needed and wanted to be making at least a six-figure income. As a kid though, I didn't know that the way to fulfilling dreams is through action – not just dreaming. I found that out the hard way!

I grew up in a family that values education – my mom has her Doctorate in education and was the superintendent of a district – yet I dropped out of high school basically because I lost my dream: I identified as a football jock and an athlete. I thought that was going to be my road to wealth. All my friends were athletes too. But then I got injured and could no longer play football. The injury I suffered resulted in the loss of my football friends along with my drive to do anything, and ultimately my dream...I felt lost. I started skipping classes, then finally dropped out.

EVEN THOUGH I WAS BORN GOOD, I ALWAYS WANTED TO BE GREAT

Eventually, I regained some of my drive. I got my GED and went on to college. I got a job delivering pizzas to help me get through college. It didn't take long to realize that delivering pizzas probably wasn't going to help me achieve the dream of true wealth. It was obvious that I needed a real job, so I started looking. One day, I noticed on the college career board a posting for a real estate assistant opening. When we were 14 and 15 years old, my brother and I, after reading *Rich Dad Poor Dad,* knew that we wanted to learn real estate investing. What that book taught us is that real estate investing is how the richest of the rich make it. I thought, what better way to learn the real estate business than to go to work and get paid as an assistant to a real estate broker. I interviewed and much to my surprise, I got the job.

In 2007, I graduated from college, got married, and bought my first house all within a span of 45 days. Around the same time, the real estate broker I was working for offered me a full-time salaried position commission-based job. Instead of jumping at that opportunity, I asked him if I could make six-figures as a 100% commission based real estate agent in my first year. He told me I could. I turned down the salaried offer and I went 100% commission based. Remember, this is 2007, and I had just gotten married and bought a house. Surprise! Despite my enthusiasm and youthful energy, I DID NOT MAKE SIX FIGURES IN MY FIRST YEAR! In fact, I only sold three homes!

Oh, but the next year, in 2008, I really started rocking and rolling! I had eight contracts getting ready to close all in one month. I was walking around, strutting my stuff like Superman. But then – SPOILER ALERT – the 2008 crash and recession happened. And yes, I lost all eight contracts.

I literally had no money. I desperately needed another job and started looking for one during a time when more people were getting fired than hired. I went on multiple interviews. Finally, a company offered me a position for $55k a year, plus benefits, and a bonus structure that would increase my earnings. There was only one problem – I would need to work pretty much seven days a week and try to squeeze in an eighth day to realistically hit the bonus structure.

On my way home after the interview, I had a realization that kind of slapped me outside my head. In my naiveté, I had been treating my real estate business more like a part time job while expecting full time income. My light bulb moment showed me that if I were to commit the same number of hours working in my own business that the company offering me that job required to meet my bonus, I knew I could make at least $55k. In fact, I saw so clearly that if I put in the kind of effort required for me to meet their bonus structure, I had an even greater possibility of hitting my coveted six-figure income. I did not accept the job with benefits.

Instead, the next morning I started working IN my real estate business. I finally came to the realization that I was willing to work harder in my business for the income of my dreams. I embraced hard work and immediately started looking for motivated buyers and sellers, or the "low hanging fruit." My question was, "How can I get in front of motivated buyers and sellers? How could I get them to hire me as their real estate agent?"

DREAMS TURN INTO VISIONS THEN INTO REALITY

As I continued to grow and my vision became more defined, I decided to take a page from one of the greatest visionaries of all times: Walt Disney. I studied Walt's vision. He took his dream and turned it into a clear vision. What I learned is that he wrote down the results he wanted to see come to life. He drew them out and wrote about the dreams he had until they became such clear visions that he could see them in his mind's eye effortlessly. He looked at those desired results and envisioned them every single day until he was living his dream and so were millions of other people first at Disney Land, then Disney World! I started doing the same thing. Then one day, I was there. I had realized my dream of having a seven-figure income from real estate!

MONEY CHANGES HANDS WHEN PROBLEMS ARE SOLVED

As I got better at identifying the "low-hanging fruit" I had another important realization. Instead of just "selling," I discovered that money changes hands more easily when people have problems, and those problems get solved. That's when it hit me: I wasn't really in the real estate business. Instead, I was in the lead-generation business. If I was going to be a problem solver, I had to generate leads. I had to be 'on the hunt', so to speak for new agents to help, new problems to solve. This turned me into a continuous 'learner'. I made a commitment to maintain what is often referred to as "beginner's mind." I resist the temptation to feel as though I've reached the pinnacle. There is always someone with a new problem to solve in a new way, always something to be learned. One expression I love and remind myself of frequently is: I don't know what I don't know! I surround myself with mentors, in the form of books, coaches, and people who have gone before me and paved the way. I love meeting and getting to know people who know more than I do, people who have achieved more than I've achieved, people who have helped in ways I can't yet fathom. While I maintain a student mind and know there's more to learn, I continuously strive for wisdom and a deeper understanding of life.

KNOW YOUR NUMBERS TO GET THE RESULTS YOU DESIRE AND DESERVE

Business is about knowing a few numbers that serve as a kind of map to achieve your goals. First, you determine how many people you need to reach out to, say in a week or a month. For instance, I know that if I reach out to 100 people, I'm going to reach at least 10. That will result in one or two appointments/ opportunities. So, I determine how many opportunities I want to schedule each week or month. It's simple math, even though it's not necessarily easy to keep reaching out and being on the hunt for new leads. But, like everything else, it gets easier with practice.

ALWAYS A STUDENT, NEVER A KNOW-IT-ALL

When you dedicate yourself to being a lifelong student, you will always find that you are expanding your abilities and your capacity to help others. You will never run out of opportunities to learn something new. For instance, I learned that to make a person feel confident in your ability has less to do with what you say than how you say it. The tone of your voice communicates more than your words do. So, have you ever thought about that? Have you ever considered how you speak to others – the tone you use – and the effect that might have on their confidence in you? People respond more to the tone you use when you speak than to the words you speak. So, you see, there's always more you can learn about yourself and the affect you have on others. You can become the person who more people trust to help them solve their problems. If you stop learning, you stop growing. If you stop growing, your business stops growing.

An example of this occurred a few years ago when my brother, Austin, who was my best friend and my business partner suddenly departed from this world. I was in shock and disbelief. Austin and I worked like magic together from the time we were teenagers. That's when we started trying to buy houses. Through this experience we found out that we were better together than we were individually. Austin had skills I did not possess and vice versa. My brother was the detail oriented one of the team. I am more a natural salesperson, while Austin understood investing and the money side of business. He was the creator and implementor for the systems that we sill use today which is why we have been able to build out such successful businesses.

After Austin was gone, I had to learn what he had been doing. I had to start from ground zero because I literally knew nothing about that side of the business. I am still in the early stages of learning about the side of the business my brother handled. I am doing it all now as a perpetual student in honor of my brother. It isn't easy, but it gets easier with practice. The student mentality keeps me from ever thinking I'm a 'know-it-all'. I certainly don't know all there is to know. And I never will. The one thing I do know though is that if I keep learning, keep growing and never give up, I may be able to positively touch and help, through my service, the lives of many more people.

WORKING TOWARD A GREATER GOOD

Once I achieved my goal of earning a seven-figure income in 2015, my thoughts turned to how I could help the greatest number of other people achieve their goals too. In addition, I started thinking about the legacy I might be able to leave for my children. With my brother gone, I had to keep going to carry on his legacy too, to make The Good Home Team a powerful presence throughout the country. What started out in 2009 as a two-man team is now a force of nearly 40-agents strong. Though it's not a done deal, we have plans of partnering with the right agents throughout the country. It's exciting to see how far we've come. Because selling real estate gives us the opportunity to earn the kind of money that we do, The Good Home Team has gone from flipping our first real estate investment in 2010 to now owning nearly $100,000,000.00 in real estate investments. In addition, The Good Home Team provides top-notch training and resources for those who also dream of making money to provide for themselves and leave a legacy for their loved ones.

Four Good Reasons People Want To Partner With The Good Home Team

The Good Home Team is well-known and respected in our town for the business we built helping people solve a variety of problems. More and more agents and other business owners came to us to help them solve their problems. It was only natural to create a training program providing partnership opportunities. This is how we help others reach for and achieve their life's goals. We provide the following:

1) An easy-to-follow plan to make six-figures and more
2) A business for those who want to be their own boss with revenue share, equity purchase, leadership roles, and health care plans
3) Time freedom – each person establishes their own schedule
4) Wealth building investment opportunities

In addition to the specific industry-focused training, we encourage our partner agents to continuously educate themselves on market trends and to pursue personal growth training. We focus our training on what to say, how to say it and when to say it. We encourage our partner agents to always be a student, to continue to study, tweak, and improve in everything they do. We are a proponent of Proactive Lead Generation which allows you to recession-proof your business and most importantly, to always be able to adapt with changes as they happen in the economy and real estate market.

THE GOOD NEWS KEEPS GETTING BETTER

Anyone who commits to putting in the effort to turn their dreams into visions and take the necessary steps to bring those visions to life can achieve their hearts' desires. We have hundreds of examples, like Walt Disney, who have already walked the path and have proved to us through their examples that literally anything is possible. If I did it, believe me, you can do it! This discovery has led me to now do everything I can to serve and help others make the discovery for themselves. While the principles I've discussed here and teach my partners apply to any business, I specifically help people who know they love helping people solve real estate problems, through buying, selling, and investing in real estate. It's been quite a journey in which I have overcome a multitude of challenges – starting with my early misunderstandings about the nature of dreams and how to turn them into reality. Then I overcame the heartbreaking challenge of losing my brother, my partner, my best friend.

We all face challenges no matter what we do in life. Continuing and committing to rise above the challenges, no matter what, is the story every successful person I've ever had the good fortune to meet, tells. Life's challenges make us stronger and more determined. That's the good, the bad, and the ugly truth about becoming a successful agent. If you can handle that truth, you can handle anything that comes your way. And that, my friend, is how I went from being a high school dropout, to a pizza delivery boy to making a seven-figure real estate income.

And that is how I help others who are ready to commit to their dreams go from good to great in real estate.

About Nick

Nick Good is founder of The Good Home Team and Co-Host on *The Only Real Estate Podcast Worth Listening To*. Nick entered the real estate industry in 2005, has sold over 3,000 properties, and has earned well over $6,000,000 in Commissions!

The Good Home Team has won the coveted Real Estate Team of The Year by *Real Producers Magazine* & numerous other real estate awards. Nick can be seen on the national stage speaking at real estate events regularly. He is a trusted source for delivering inspirational and educational insights about the team culture, leadership, and real estate marketing.

His passion for helping others continues to drive him in his professional career, and he is committed to taking the real estate industry to the next level and inspiring others to achieve their financial dreams through an easy-to-follow blueprint that can guarantee an agent to make six figures!

When he's not working, you can find him enjoying time with his family going skiing (or attempting to ski) or relaxing at their lake house. Nick truly enjoys helping others become successful in life and business. So, if you are looking for a success story that shows what it takes to make it big in real estate, then look no further, because The Good Home Team has got you covered!

You can learn more about Nick and The Good Home Team at:

- http://NickGood.work

CHAPTER 6

LISTINGS ARE THE KEY

BY JAY KINDER

My best year I sold 531 homes and had 12% market share. How did I do it you ask? I became the most dominant listing agent in my market. The better question for me to answer for you is – How did I get started? The answer is simple; I focused on getting listings. You see listings have babies. You have a listing and get buyers. Your seller might be buying another house. When you sell that listing you get calls from other sellers that want to sell. Listings have a compound effect on your real estate business. That's why you start here and put all your energy in finding listing opportunities and learning how to win listings when you get face-to-face with sellers.

LISTINGS PAY MORE PER HOUR

Another benefit of getting listings is that you spend less time with a seller than a buyer. On average, you spend three hours with a seller and 21 hours with a seller. That means, for the same commission you are 7X more efficient when working with a seller than with a buyer! It's the highest dollar per hour work you can do. If the goal is to build a six- or even seven-figure business like I did then you should master getting listings.

LISTINGS ALSO BUILD YOUR BRAND

Market research shows that the average person needs to see your brand 17-21 times before they 'think of you' when it comes time to sell. The more signs you have up in your market the more people that are seeing your brand. Branding is all about impressions. When someone drives by one of your signs in their neighborhood on the way to work and again on the way home that is two impressions per day. If they come home for lunch or to pick up the kids from school that's four impressions per day. Multiply that times how many days it's there.

TO GET LISTINGS YOU MUST HAVE A VALUE PROPOSITION

The first thing you must have if you want to win listings is a value proposition. Said differently, Why should someone do business with you vs. doing business with someone else. I can't teach you this in one chapter in a book so I am going to do you a solid. As co-founder of the National Association of Expert Advisors we created the Certified Home Selling Advisor (CHSA) designation that is like Navy Seal Training for listing agents. We typically only reserve this for agents that partner with us at eXp. Since someone shared this book with you, my hope is you are considering getting all the value from partnering with us so I am going to treat you as if you are already a partner. Go to Honeybadger.TRAINING to get access to the course for free. It includes a "done for you listing presentation and marketing materials positioning you as the local expert. It's a proven, repeatable system for winning listings at your price and terms without having to discount. Pure fire. We typically sell this course for $3,000 and you are getting it for free.

TWO BEST FREE SOURCES OF LISTING LEADS

There are only two free sources for getting listings that are available to you. One is For Sale By Owners (FSBO's) and the other is Expireds. Expired listings exist in hot markets and are more prevalent in markets that have shifted in favor of buyers. There are always expired listings and these sellers have proven they want to sell and are willing to pay a commission. It's also the best way to get real world repetitions on practicing the process we teach you in the CHSA course. 'For sale by owners' are also always available. There are usually more FSBO's on the market than you think. These sellers want to try to sell and save the commission, but they don't get the exposure to the most buyers since they aren't in the MLS and generally don't have the ability to market their home using the tools agents have available to them.

Having coached thousands of agents, I can tell you ALL of the agents that went on to build six- or seven-figure businesses used these two pillars to generate revenue to fuel their growth. If you focus on them you should easily be able to generate 3-4 closings a month from these two free lead sources. If the average sales price in your area is around the national average of $300,000, that's a $9,000 commission. That's $27,000-$36,000 a month or $324,000-$432,000 a year in commissions with no cost to acquire a client.

If you want access to my *How to make $500K a year with FSBO's*, you can access it for free here. Go to Honeybadger. training and download the scripts and watch the training.

If you want access to our 'How to win Expired listings' training you can also access it for free as well at *Honeybadger.training*.

The best way for you to get access to all the FSBO's and Expireds in your market is with a tool all the top agents use to get them sent to them daily. You can get access to it for a discount when you use this link: https://www.redx.com/naea/

HOW TO BUILD YOUR GEOGRAPHIC FARM AREA

A farm area is a specific geographic area where you want to focus your efforts, build your brand, and become the dominant listing agent. The most effective way to build a farm is to look at the turnover rates in a given area. How many homes are in that particular area divided into how many homes sold in the last 12 months. Neighborhoods with a 10% minimum should be the goal. So if there are 1,000 homes in your target area and 70 sold in the last 12 months that means you have the potential target market of 70 sellers per year. If you capture 10% market share that would be 7 homes sold. At one point I had nearly 50% of market share in my target market and I have seen agents accomplish as much as 85% market share of a particular neighborhood.

Once you have selected a target market, the next step is to determine how you will get to 21 impressions over what period of time, and what medium you will use to do that. The number one reason why agents don't have success farming is they underestimate the number of impressions it takes to become 'top of mind'. If you mailed something once a quarter then it would take you over 5 years to become top of mind. I would argue that it would never work. They just don't see you enough. My suggestion is you use direct mail weekly for 12 weeks straight and then move to twice a month. That's a total of 28 mailings per year. If your average cost is $2.50 per mailer you are investing $70 per house. If there are 1,000 homes with a 10% turnover rate that would be 100 homes or 1 out of 10 that sell. If you capture 10% your first year (10 listings sold) you would be investing $560 per home sold. You do the math. Your average sales price x your average commission percentage with a cost of $560 is a great return on investment.

BUSINESS ASSUMPTIONS FOR YOUR FARM

- 28 mailings x $2.50 = $70
- 1,000 homes x $70 = $7,000
- Monthly investment = $583/month
- Farm turnover rate = 10%
- Annual home sales = 100
- Target Capture rate = 10%
- Listings taken/sold = 10
- Average Sales Price = $350,000
- Average Commission = 2.8%
- Average Commission $ 9,800
- Annual commission earned =$98,000
- ROI = 1,400%

These assumptions don't count any referrals, new listings, or buyers you close from having these listings which boost your actual ROI up even higher. That makes this one of the highest ROI activities you could execute on in your business.

WHAT DO YOU MAIL

My suggestion is jumbo postcards with your brand. You want to mix in just solds, testimonials, and market data to be professionally relevant and market area relevant. Be sure to follow the rules of direct response marketing with each postcard. They are as follows:

The Rules of Direct Response

- It must have an OFFER
- Reason to Respond NOW
- Tell them what to do
- Tracking and accountability
- Only no-cost branding
- Follow-up process
- Strong copy
- Results Rule

For an example of a postcard that follows the rules of direct response marketing, you can see it at: *honeybadger.training/ postcard*

If you want to know the secret to $100,000, $500,000 or even a multi-seven-figure real estate business focus on getting listings. and remember, it's not the best real estate agent that sells the most homes – *it's the best marketer.*

About Jay

Jay Kinder is CEO and co-founder of the National Association of Expert Advisors and co-host of the popular podcast, *Face to Face* with Jay Kinder and Michael Reese. Together they are taking their proven track records as successful mega agents and are doing what nobody else in the real estate industry has been willing to do—focusing on agent productivity. In the 127 Billion dollar real estate industry, where none of the major brands manage the customer experience, they have carved out a niche by doing what Steve Jobs found to be true: *Saying 'no' more than saying 'yes'.*

While most companies have focused on eliminating the ever-so-resilient real estate agent they've aligned with them, they decided to only focus on agents that have set out to be the local expert. By partnering with agents, they have been able to add more value to those agents, ramping up their businesses to market dominating positions. It's working too, as the *Inc. 5000* has awarded them one of the fastest growing companies in America for six years in a row.

Jay Kinder is a real estate entrepreneur who went from small-town kid to master business growth strategist recognized throughout the real estate industry. Nobody in the tiny town of Walters, Oklahoma, population 2,142, would have voted this notably 'ornery' and average student most likely to succeed, but that didn't stop him from building an impressive real estate brand – positioning him as the #2 Coldwell Banker Agent Worldwide, Small Business Administration Young Entrepreneur of the Year, *Realtor* magazine's 30 under 30, *The Wall Street Journal*'s top 25 agents worldwide, and a laundry list of high achievement awards all by the age of 30 years old. By the time Jay was 25 years old, he had become a local celebrity and commanded 14% market share of all home sales in his area.

By the time he was 28, his passion for real estate expanded as he and his business partner Michael Reese, a top agent that got into real estate after seeing Jay's incredible business success, decided to open the doors of a new business together. They began recreating their own success by helping agents like themselves master massive growth and celebrity stardom in their own real estate markets. Through the National Association of Expert Advisors, they have been credited with helping thousands of real estate agents strategically grow their businesses with their proven, market-tested ideas. Jay and Michael have had a simple philosophy of adding value to people's lives.

In November of 2017, they made a move that nobody saw coming. Priding themselves on being radically open-minded and always seeking a better way, they partnered with longtime friend and client Al Stasek, and joined eXp Realty where together they are growing their enterprise in the U.S. and Canada with Global expansion on the horizon. This partnership has allowed them to completely align with agents that want to grow their business and take advantage of the unparalleled revenue share program offered exclusively through eXp Realty.

CHAPTER 7

DEVELOPING THE DISCIPLINE TO ACHIEVE YOUR DESIRED OUTCOME

BY JOHN KITCHENS

The journey towards becoming a 6-figure agent is no easy feat. The higher we step into the ladder, the greater the challenge. To many of us, climbing toward the next level feels like a long-winded battle. We do all the things we know how to get there, yet we still find ourselves in the same cycle of wishing for a breakthrough. Will it ever be different? What does it take to transform our struggles into wins? What do we need to do in order to live the life that we desire and a life that we deserve?

To be truly honest, the answer is not a farfetched one. It lies within ourselves. Reaching the next level is not about some big idea or some hidden secret waiting to be unlocked. There is no secret. There is no magic. It all boils down to developing discipline and significant habits to achieve your desired outcome. Behavior is the powerful force that shapes our habits and drives our results. When we develop habits that push us forward, we take a step closer to our goals. It is not always easy. The level of commitment and effort that goes into developing the discipline is immense. Yet there are people who expect to come out successful when they don't even have a basic understanding of what drives their results. They tend to blindly go at bigger things when it's the small habits that matter the most.

Remember that we don't rise to the level of our expectations, we fall to the level of our training. We have to understand that to achieve our desired outcome, it requires discipline to constantly train ourselves with habits that will drive our results.

BUILDING SUCCESS HABITS

In a 2002 study by USC psychologist and habit researcher, Dr. Wendy Wood, it is revealed that 43% of what people do every day is habitual. We eat, sleep, take a bath, change our clothes, and do many more things on repeat. Through repetition, these everyday things become ingrained in our daily lives and we acquire the ability to execute them with little to no effort. This can only mean that learning significant habits will give us an automatic and effortless response to achieving our goals. And it is totally possible to create habits that lead us to success, yet why are people having difficulty building these success habits?

The factors can include the following:

1. Lack of knowledge or understanding about the potential benefits it offers.
2. A belief that habits are difficult to create or break and thus not worth investing effort in.
3. Difficulty finding motivation in changing their habits.
4. The fear of trying something new.
5. A lack of structure or support when embarking on new lifestyle changes.

People often neglect the benefits of a good habit because it takes discipline and dedication to stick with it. Good habits require regular, consistent effort and many people struggle with maintaining motivation as well as developing an effective system for tracking progress. Additionally, making changes can be uncomfortable and unfamiliar, which can cause individuals to shy away from trying something new even if it could benefit them in the long run. But if you follow an effective framework of habits, you will definitely be able to learn the habits that will drive your business to the next level.

THE PROCESS

The best way to predict your future is to create it.
~ Abraham Lincoln

Creating habits that drive our business is not an overnight affair. It requires courage to be committed to the process and to have discipline in order to make it a reality. The step-by-step process to creating habits that drive our business success is as follows:

(i). Set a Known Direction

A journey without a destination is a journey without purpose. This applies to any equity of our lives. Whether it is our relationships, health, or business, we need to know our desired outcome in order to get there. Without a goal, we can't really tell what steps we should be taking to move us toward our destination.

You need to have a point A and a point B.

Take the time to think of your vision and be specific. It has to be clear and concise with an aim of reaching something specific at the end. You have to get clear on what the goal is and why you're doing it. When you have a clear goal in mind, you'll know what success looks like and you will have a clear idea of where you want to be and how you can get there. Once your goals are set, you will now be able to identify the steps you need to take to get there.

71

(ii). Establish The Plan

Now that your goal has been set, it's time to plan what activities you should be doing to move closer to your goal. Identifying those activities requires you to consider the amount of money or revenue that you wanted to make. Then, you have to reverse engineer what it's going to take to achieve your desired outcome from an activity standpoint. So you have to break down your goals into measurable pieces. Then you have to make sure that you get dialed in on what it takes to win the quarter, the month, the week, and the day. This way, you are able to get a clear target for each period and establish the appropriate activities that will deliver results. By planning ahead, you are able to set yourself up for success and stay on track.

(iii). Apply It To Your Calendar

Now that you've set your goal and established your plan, all that's left to do is to apply it in your daily life. What better way to do this than to put habits into our calendar? Habits form through repetition and that means applying these habits to your daily routine is of utmost importance. Setting up your calendar allows you to maximize the time and really focus on the right things in the right order. This process is proven to help people successfully achieve their goals and win in business and in life. We want to review and set our calendar each week to ensure that habits are being done consistently and as planned.

How do you know what activities should go into your calendar?

First, we have to separate our activities into 4 different categories:

a) HLVA – High Lifetime Value Activities
b) Non-Negotiables – Activities that are a must
c) HLA – High Leverage Activities
d) MVP – Most Valuable Priorities

The first step is where a lot of people mess up. They often prioritize work over other activities; however, this method goes against the concept of the Right Things in the Right Order.

So what activities should go into the calendar first?

The right thing that goes into your calendar first is the activities that are High Lifetime Value Activities (HLVA). HLVAs are activities that focus on long-term goals, rather than short-term gratification. These activities can have a significant positive impact on your life, in terms of both overall well-being and financial security.

Examples of High Lifetime Value Activities include:

o Meditation
o Reading
o Learning new skills
o Spending time in deepening relationships

The second activity that goes into your calendar should be Non-negotiables. Non-negotiable activities are tasks that should be completed regularly and cannot be skipped. These activities are typically necessary for success and involve something that you value highly.

Examples of non-negotiable activities include:

o Date Night
o Fitness
o Time with Family
o Self-care

The next activity that goes into your calendar should be High Leverage Activities(HLA). HLAs are activities that result in the most growth and impact with the least amount of time and effort. These activities produce the most benefit with the least amount of effort and are typically activities that require specialized knowledge or special skills.

Examples of High Leverage Activities include:

- Lead Generation
- Lead Conversion
- Face-to-Face articulating your value
- Showing Properties
- Negotiating Deals
- Building your Brand

For the next one, we have the Most Valuable Priorities (MVPs) or the three most valuable things that need to progress within the week. MVPs are activities that you prioritize over all other activities. These are goals that you commit to achieving each week and should be highly focused on during that time. Ideally, allocating 90 minutes to each of your MVPs should be enough to make significant progress.

Examples of MVPs are:

- Developing a business plan
- Writing content for marketing
- Creating a budget

After adding activities from the four categories, you can add other significant activities that need to be accomplished to your calendar.

Examples of this are:

> Workout Schedule
> Meal Schedule
> Kids Schedule
> Social Media Content Schedule

What activities shouldn't go on your calendar?

There are activities that should NOT be added to your calendar. These are activities such as scrolling through social media or playing video games and other habits that create distraction and uncertainty. These are activities that do not provide long-term benefits and can be detrimental to your habits and success. Being disciplined with the calendar does not only mean that you complete your tasks, but it also means having the discipline to avoid activities that would divert you from achieving your goals. Let us stop chasing shiny objects that peel us away from our priorities. If it's not in your calendar, then it doesn't happen.

By aligning habits to your calendar, you are able to condition yourself to take on a systematic approach to achieving the desired outcome over time. It also allows us to have more control over our habits so that we can measure their progress more accurately. The discipline of setting your calendar allows you to be constantly reminded of your goals and how to achieve them. This does not only align your habits, but it also creates the rhythm that you need to increase your success rate and productivity.

BASIC PRINCIPLES YOU SHOULD REMEMBER

To properly develop the discipline of driving your results, you have to remember some basic things that go with the process. You can only execute the process once you understand the following:

1. Show Up better than what anybody expected

"Nobody will truly value you until you truly value yourself first."

Showing up and putting in the effort to become better than what your expectations are is one of the basic things that we shouldn't forget. Even if we don't feel like it, we owe it to ourselves to show up with our best. Not for the sake of others but for ourselves. And for us to play on any next level in any equity of our life, we've got to be willing to make the commitment to show up no matter what. This helps us build and develop the success habits that we need to live the life we desire.

75

2. Surround Yourself with the Right People

Surrounding yourself with the right people can have a huge impact on your life and success. Having positive, like-minded individuals that are passionate about achieving their goals are essential. We also need to make sure that the people we're surrounding ourselves with are those people who are telling us what we need to hear, not what we want to hear. The right people are not only keeping you in check but are also lifting you up – reminding you to believe that you've got what it takes to make it to the next level. This will inspire growth and help you be accountable for your habits and success.

3. Put in the Work

Taking things to the next level takes more than just saying you want to do it. We should be willing to make sacrifices and put in the work because there is no silver bullet. There is no magic pill. *The magic pill is hard work.* We've got to be willing to make sacrifices to change our behavior, to change our habits. That's where people get left behind. They're not willing to make sacrifices with their time, money, and relationships. And that's what will hold people back from achieving things. If we want to become the best in the industry, we have to take the initiative and put in the work.

Anything that we want in our life that's at a pro level, we are not going to get there with amateur habits. It's not enough just to set goals and wait for them to manifest. You need the discipline of habits in order to achieve your desired outcome. Your effort, your hard work, and your sacrifice have to match in order for you to become a six-figure agent.

After all, success is not a destination, it's a lifestyle.

About John

John Kitchens is the most sought-after business growth and leadership development coach for real estate agents that want to build a sustainable business. John helps people become the best versions of themselves. He helps clients turn their real estate practice into a business which allows them to have an actionable plan – to escape being a production agent and become the CEO and leader of their business.

Breaking apart goals into actionable systems and processes is what defines him. Whether it's an Ironman finish, creating an organizational structure, or self-leadership principles through his consistency, daily disciplines, and habits, he helps identify and focus on the details that are vital, will lead to success, and make big things happen. With over 14,000 coaching calls, his experience and broad perspective in all of the business dynamics allow him to bring clarity no other coach can.

Today, John is constantly traveling to speak and create an impact to transform people's lives. He also leads his own team and has created structured coaching programs to xXelerate your business and xXelerate your life.

John believes the only thing easier than getting a real estate license is saying you're a coach. That's why he created the Coach Code Coaching Certification program for those who truly want to coach. This program gives you the foundation and framework to be a world-class coach in today's environment.

He lives by his 'WHY':

Inspire and challenge people to think bigger so they can transform their business and transform their lives.

CHAPTER 8

THE BENEFIT OF JOINING A TEAM

BY SHELLY SALAS

"Making 6 figures, are you insane!...That's not possible in my area!

He/She can do it because...(insert all my excuses)."

These were the thoughts I had for many years when I first got into real estate. Having this mindset didn't allow me to think past the end of my nose. You see, in my area, the median income for families was about $30k/year and the average sales price of a home was less than $150k. Making six figures seemed impossible to me. But what I didn't realize is that I was actually setting limitations on what I could do.

We are typically the ones who set our own limitations. No one can stop us from achieving what we want once we set our minds to it. I was no different once I changed my mindset to: "Well wait a minute! If it works in their market, why can't it work in mine." And once I started thinking, "Well if they can do it, why can't I?"...then it all started coming together.

Many of you are probably in the same place that I was many

years ago – thinking that it's impossible to make six figures. I'm not going to lie, it is tough, it requires hustle, grind and commitment to not only yourself, but also to your business and your clients. Depending on your market average sales price, it may require more homes to be sold or more families that need to be served, but the point is it's definitely achievable.

I have many members on my team that are not just grossing six figures, they are netting six figures every year, and our average sales price is only about $230k!

Throughout the years, I built systems and processes that helped me achieve my goals and I now share and train all my team on how to use these tips so they can quickly get to six figures—instead of going through all the headaches I went through. I love coaching my team and watching their success. Watching them achieve their goals is truly a gratifying and humbling experience that I love doing.

Why re-invent the wheel? Why go through all the trials and tribulations of creating a process, systems, etc. when I'm sure there's one already out there? Save yourselves the headaches, grey hairs and unnecessary stress of trying to build something that already exists. This doesn't mean you can't 'tweak' what is already there, it simply means you get on the moving bus, not the parked bus.

When I first started in real estate, what I have now was not out there…at least that I'm aware of. My system and processes evolved throughout the years. These processes changed every time the market changed, and my systems changed as my team grew as well. I discovered that you can outgrow your own system. Once I realized this, I brought some of my leadership team into the room and we quickly "tweaked" our processes and system. As we serve more and more families every year, we discover that the system and processes we have in place today may not give us the outcome we were seeking tomorrow.

This is why we are constantly auditing our own processes and systems. We want to make sure our client experience does not suffer because of a changing market or growing team.

This requires a lot of time and effort taking you away from what you really enjoy – which is working with people. I believe that if you're in this career, a sales career, I'm assuming you love working with people. (If you don't, I hate to say it but you may want to consider another career, LOL.) I know I absolutely love it. I love meeting new people; I love helping our clients achieve the American Dream of home ownership. I love helping our seller clients get top dollar for their home and start life's new chapter wherever that may be for them. This is why I was so focused on creating a great process to make sure our clients always walked away with our *2nd Mile Service*. They deserved this.

Being a solo/single agent out there in today's market is hard. And quite honestly, I believe it's a thing of the past. There are so many teams out there that have spent the man hours, the sweat and the tears, as well as feeling the frustration it takes to build a team, that they are dominating prospective markets. As a solo agent, it's hard to focus on clients while trying to create all the systems and processes needed to start building a team. It's not impossible, you can obviously do it as I did but go ahead and say goodbye to any personal life, because that's what this takes. It takes a significant amount of sacrifice on your part, not just from you though, if you have a family or are in a relationship, but it's kind of their sacrifice as well. I say this because when you put your time into anything it's being taken away from somewhere else.

So my question becomes why? Why would you want to do this on your own? Why would you want to put not only yourself, but also your friends and family through this journey? It is difficult to fund a business with new clients when simultaneously trying to develop the systems you need—NOT IMPOSSIBLE...but difficult! Again, when I first started, real estate teams were really unheard of. They simply weren't out there. And the ones that did exist were really a team by name only. At least that was my personal experience. Being a solo agent was the way it was done; it was the norm at the time, but not today. Like any industry, things change, industries evolve with the times.

I look back and man, do I wish there would've been a team like mine when I first joined. I would've joined that team and simply 'plugged and played'. I could have reached so many of my personal and professional goals a lot quicker. I surely would have given myself less grey hairs and wrinkles, LOL.

There's a lot of leverage being on a team. Well, to be clear, there's a lot of great leverage if you're on the right team—an actual team that has the data to back up what they are saying. I have heard from many members on my team that there are many 'teams' out there by name only, not by their actions. But if you are on a true team, your career can go where you want it to go a heck of a lot quicker. You can reach your first six digits in months not years. Heck yeah! Sign me up. If I can reach my goal quicker, why not. If I can have a successful career quicker, why not? It would be silly of me not too!

When we have someone from another Brokerage requesting to join my team, one of the first things we do is ask them "Why?" Why do they want to be on a team now when they've been doing it on their own for the past year or two (or sometimes longer), and you know what they say, "It's hard out there."

Marketing is expensive, it's hard to follow-up with old leads while trying to generate new ones, and on top of all this, you're trying to squeeze the time in to show or list homes for existing clients—while managing your own 'under contract/pending' clients. Yeah, it's a lot for one person to do on their own. Basically, they said they were somewhat successful but not where they wanted to truly be. They wanted a career they could be proud of and to provide a certain lifestyle for their family while having more free time on their hands.

It's my personal belief that as a new agent you should definitely join a team. But honestly, not just a new agent, but really anyone in the industry that is tired or stressed out by having to handle all aspects of a real estate transaction on their own. You have to do your research though, there's too many teams out there to choose from. How will the team you are considering help you reach your goals? Make sure you are asking them questions so you can empower yourself with good information and make a logical decision that makes sense for you.

Here is a list of the top five questions you should definitely ask at your interview:

1. Will you provide training? If so. what does that look like?
2. Will you be providing me with appointments?
3. Will I have marketing expenses while on your team?
4. Do you have a closing department that will help facilitate my closings?
5. Tell me about your culture?

You should feel comfortable enough to ask these questions at your next team interview. This is your career; you should want the best for yourself.

I added the culture question because I think all successful teams should have a great culture. A great culture says a lot about any organization or team. Culture plays a huge role in your success. They kind of go hand in hand. When employees are happy to go to work, it's felt in the office environment. That feeling is carried over and felt by the customers/clients that enter that particular business environment. I personally wouldn't want to work in an environment where there's drama, unhappiness or a 'backstabbing' type of attitude. I want to work in a place where we can be happy for each other's success, collaborate openly with each other, and push each other to reach our goals.

When you have this type of culture, trust me, the customers/clients walking through the doors of that business will feel it and they will want to work with those people. So don't forget to ask about their culture.

As I wrap up this chapter, I hope that I have shown you that there is much value in joining a team, but to be clear, not just any team. Make sure you are doing thorough research on any team you plan to interview with. This is your career. Invest in yourself from the get-go. If you do the leg work in the beginning it definitely will pay off in your near future. Once you join the team, write your goal down on paper and don't lose sight of it. Post it in front of you, look at it daily. How many families do you need to serve in order to reach your six-figure income goal. Don't get distracted by the nonsense that sometimes happens in this industry. Stay away from the drama that tends to sometimes surround many agents in this field. While on your new team, make sure you are attending all live training sessions they offer. This should be a great opportunity for you to walk away with at least one good nugget, one good idea that you can implement in your business.

Make sure you are collaborating with the top producers of your team. Shadow them, ask them questions, learn from them. What they are doing is obviously working, so why not do what they are doing. Don't be afraid to ask questions. A true team will want you to improve your sales skills so you can be successful in your career. I'm always telling my team that we are as strong as our weakest link. I really do believe in the saying, 'A rising tide raises all boats.' As a team leader, nothing fills my heart more than watching all of our team members fulfilling their goals—both personal and business goals. Knowing that I had something to do with their growth and success is priceless, humbling and gratifying for me.

I want to help everyone reach their first six-figures in real estate, so this way everyone can be living their best life – whatever that looks like for them. We all have a different definition of what success looks like...debt free, traveling the world, building wealth through real estate, building an amazing legacy for their family or just simply having more free time. However success looks like to you, I can assure you that you can reach your success a 'heck of a lot quicker' while on a great team rather than being a solo agent. And you can have tons of fun along the way in this career if the culture is right! Life can't get any better than this!

About Shelly

Shelly Salas is the Team Leader of the number one team in Central Texas. She went from being a solo agent alongside her husband, working with bank-owned properties to helping thousands of families get into or out of a home. She has been ranked the #1 Agent in the United States according to NAHREP in 2021. She has consistently ranked in the top 1% in the Nation as advertised in *The Wall Street Journal* Real Trends ranking report and America's Best Real Estate Professionals. Shelly has been a member of the Zillow Agent Advisory Board for the past two years and is on the McLane Children's Medical Center Advisory Council.

As an Army Veteran she is able to apply the leadership skills she gained while in service to train her team, and she also applies her gained knowledge from her Psychology degree when mentoring her team and analyzing and solving a problem.

Not only does Shelly help clients buy and sell real estate, but she is also an investor herself. She has flipped many homes throughout her career. She is still actively buying and selling real estate for her own real estate portfolio. She uses her experience and knowledge of investing and shares this knowledge with her team and investor clients.

Shelly also co-authored two Best-Selling Books, *Real Estate Game Changers* and *Pay It Forward*. She is also the host of the *Shelly Salas Real Estate Show*. The radio show streams live every Saturday and Sunday on KTEM 1400 and FM 94.3. Shelly owes her work ethic to her upbringing, working since she was a child in the orange, cucumber, and watermelon fields from sunup to sundown. She definitely never shies away from working long hours when needed. Her joy in life is helping other people reach their hearts desire, whether it is a team member or a client.

Shelly loves to give back. Every year, together with her team, she donates thousands to the Children's Miracle Network, and together they also give individually-wrapped Christmas gifts to thousands of children in very low-income areas each year.

Shelly has been married for over 23 years to her husband Luis and together they have three wonderful children – Bryonna, Louis and Michael. Real Estate is her passion, but her family is her life.

You can connect with Shelly at:

- shelly@thesalasteam.com
- www.facebook.com/thesalasteamrealtors
- www.Instagram.com/thesalasteamrealtors
- www.shellysalas.com

CHAPTER 9

THREE LITTLE HACKS THAT CHANGED EVERYTHING

BY NICKI GREGORY KOCH

My journey to become a six-figure agent was not a linear one. And it began when I was a young girl around the age of 12. I knew a few things already about myself. I knew that I had a head full of ideas, and most of them were the entrepreneurial kind.

I don't believe it was a coincidence that this was also the age that my dad, who was a missionary, decided it was time to expose me to what many parts of the rest of the world looked like. So, he packed me up...and for the next few years, we took trips to the most impoverished parts of Central America. On these trips, I saw with my own eyes what others usually only hear about or see on television or portrayed in movies. I saw thousands of people, from babies to the elderly – living on the streets and in cardboard box huts. We traveled to remote mountain villages where I played with other children my same age who had nothing to eat. I made friends with a little boy who had no parents, no guardians at all...he would sit with me and eat leaves from the trees...I think that's all he ever knew.

I would travel back home and see the stark contrast of our world...and some things began to become very clear to me... mostly that I was born with extreme opportunity, just by being lucky enough to be born in this country. And with that came responsibility, and not just to 'not screw it up' or waste it...there seemed to be much more to it than that.

It was clear to me that anyone lucky enough to have this much opportunity must also be responsible enough to take what has been given to them and grow it big enough to also help those who aren't in the same position. I quickly came to believe that anyone whose mind is flooded with entrepreneurial ideas, and who was born with things like thick skin, leadership and people skills, and a talent for building things and improving on things others have built...those people have an actual calling to be successful, not just for them and their family...but to impact the entire world. As I got older and the more conversations I had with successful people the more my belief was confirmed... they can feel it in their bones...they know they are different in a profound and big way...but most of them are constantly searching for why.

Later, as an adult I found myself in real estate...(here's where the non-linear part comes in) and in all of the ups and downs that often come with that career path. Despite that though...I did eventually find myself on a path that appeared successful to those around me. At this point, however, I had bought into a few lies...lies that didn't align with my definition of success. So, although others could see the 'pretty' life I lead, the beautiful new house I designed and lived in, located in the neighborhood all my clients dreamed of living in, the impeccably dressed kids, the brand names, the seemingly great marriage...behind the scenes there was chaos.

Although there is nothing wrong with having 'things' (things are not inherently good or bad, they are simply things) I didn't find happiness there. And we all know that having relationships can be fulfilling but having them for the wrong reasons or with the wrong person will most certainly be devastating in the end.

And then there was my business. Nothing in my business aligned with my core beliefs or why I felt I was put on this planet, so the foundation was completely non-existent...and as a result...things were always 2 steps forward and 18 steps back. Needless to say,...it all came crashing down. Hard! And I found myself starting over.

Although it was through absolute and unbearable heartache...I now, at the very least, had a clean slate. A foundation on which to rebuild. The difference this time was the gift of hindsight, which meant I could create the life I wanted, with the kind of success that was meaningful to me.

A clean slate doesn't mean starting from square one, so, I knew that I needed to rebuild quickly – and it needed to last! So, I started to look for simple ways to 'hack the system'.

I want to share the top three 'hacks' I discovered on this journey that can help you avoid a life crash and instead collapse time and expedite your journey to lasting fulfillment and financial success. The first step is always the hardest, but in many ways is also the simplest, you just need to take the leap. The same is true for these three hacks:

Hack #1 – *Get in better rooms with better conversations.*

This is the first right thing I did to get back on top of my life and my success.

In the thralls of separation and what became an ugly divorce, I became overwhelmingly mentally and emotionally exhausted. I found myself with a low support system at home, I was feeling judged, and was tired of questioning my own decisions. Losing a 21-year marriage and a second income was terrifying and paralyzing, but I couldn't be paralyzed. I had three children and a life to take care of, so I needed to find a way to up my income and do it NOW.

I remembered the advice of a past mentor. He told me that if and when I ever found myself frustrated in my career, look for better rooms with better conversations and get in them—at all costs. And then, I was invited to a mastermind for people in real estate and knew that this was my ticket up. The answer I had been looking for, and I needed to do whatever it took to get in that room. So, I did.

On the first day of the mastermind, I walked in, and almost walked out. Self-doubt crept in, my subconscious began to sabotage me, and imposter syndrome hit hard! I didn't feel like I fit in, but I knew I had to tough it out. Once I made the decision to stick it out, something magical happened—I had done it. This was it. As much as I could hear myself screaming in my head "I am in the wrong room" it became more and more clear...I was in THE EXACT RIGHT room I needed to change everything!

I listened to extraordinary conversations where no idea was off-limits. I began to share my own thoughts, dreams, ideas... everything that had been shut down; stifled, called stupid, impossible, silly...in THIS room all I heard was, "I love it," "You should do it," "How can I help you?" and "How can WE make that happen?" I felt like I had won the lottery. This wasn't just a better room with better conversations - it was the BEST room with the BEST conversations.

In this moment, I was living what my mentor taught me many years before: The atmosphere I chose to put myself in was the #1 priority, and the very first piece of the puzzle to my success and will be to yours too.

Hack #2 – *Assign money a purpose, and the purpose will attract the money.*

If you've ever been in a mastermind or real estate training or coaching, you've probably been asked, "What is your 5 or 10-year goal?" When asked, my answer over the years was always the same, "To be the #1 agent in my market." And they never questioned me, to them that answer was good enough. When I leveled up the rooms and the conversations...I also leveled up who my mentors and coaches were, and they did not settle for "good enough."

It didn't take long for my new coach to ask me the question, "Nicki, what is your goal?" Like always, I answered, "To be the #1 agent in my market." He responded, "Really, that's it?" He didn't settle for my basic answer and after a few minutes of coaching, I discovered my real answer: To make six figures to comfortably cover my living expenses and start my own nonprofit to combat child trafficking.

I had already been donating some money from each closing to organizations fighting against human trafficking, but this was the first time I had verbalized my deepest desire to do something bigger. When I spoke those words, it struck me like lightning: my success, the money, the six figures were the journey, not the destination.

I had been making money the goal, and that was what was creating my struggle. The goal was too vague, it didn't have enough definition because it wasn't connected to the core of what would make me feel fulfilled. I was struggling to create any steady financial growth and could finally see that it was the lack of clear direction for my money. Money is just a tool. It can do nothing alone. Its only function is to serve its master.

Money's master is purpose. Without direction it will sift through your fingers like sand. It will never bring you happiness and, as the song goes, 'money can't buy you love'. But when money is used as a tool to serve a purpose, the doors of opportunity open and your life will take on a new shape. This simple shift in mindset turned into more clients, agents joining my team and financial burdens were being lifted. By focusing on giving my money a purpose and living a fulfilling life, I attracted success to me.

It changed my life so much that within the first year of starting this mastermind and changing my thinking, not only was my business more successful than ever, but I was also able to build a functioning non-profit that raised money to fight child trafficking by utilizing an automated system that didn't require all of my time.

By giving my money focus and purpose, I found myself having to come up with a new 10-year goal because I achieved my first one in 12 months!

Hack #3 – *Get to give so you can give to get...and then repeat!* (The key is to keep it all in motion.)

I am most excited about sharing this hack with you because it is the key to exponential growth and transformation. In fact, this is more than just a hack, it's a life principle:

Things that flow, live. Things that don't, die.

- Blood flows through our veins, the heart takes the blood and then pumps it out back out into the body to keep it flowing at all times. The process repeats to keep us alive.
- Air flows into our lungs, oxygen then flows to the blood, carbon dioxide flows from the blood to the lungs, and then is exhaled back out.

If this process stops, we die.

Money works by the same principle…money in, money out. Money in again, money out again. Rinse and repeat. Those that are good stewards of the money that comes in and put it back into the world in a responsible and healthy manner, will continually be entrusted to oversee the survival of this precious resource.

We all define success differently, and this life principle in action will look different for every person. I am not here to judge or condemn material things and the desire for wealth, but I believe that it is our responsibility as humans with certain gifts and talents to use the resources we have by putting back into the world what we have received. By not holding on too tightly to resources, and sharing what we have with others, we open ourselves up to receive more, not less.

I do believe that there are individuals on this planet that are put here with an absolute calling to bring in money and do things with that money that will change the world for the better. Whether that's by starting businesses and creating jobs or donating to help others. We should seek to do our best, make the most we can, and give as much as we can to help others.

The key is to keep the money flowing and to keep it healthy… to not let it become dead and stagnant by spending or wasting it on things that will cause it to do so. It is different for each of us, but it is our responsibility to look within and see where we can breathe life into the resources we have and put it back into the world with passion and purpose. When you do this, opportunity will come back to you, over and over again, because you have proven you can be trusted with it.

An open hand does not just give more, an open hand has more room to receive.

When I started operating this way, it attracted like-minded people to me. And in living this life of giving to others and collaborating with like-minded people, success became inevitable. It was as if I couldn't help but succeed. All by incorporating these three simple hacks, my life changed forever. Everything that was so hard for so long came with ease and exponential growth.

So, that's it...these are the three things that I lovingly refer to as "hacks" I am gifting to you. If you're reading this book because you're struggling and need answers, try them for yourself:

- Go out today and find a better room with better conversations.
- Assign the money a purpose and write it somewhere big and highly visible.
- Allow what money you bring in to flow and live, don't let it become stagnant and die. Send it back out into the world with a higher purpose.

You have all the information that changed my life...what you do with it now is up to you!

I want to wish you all the success in the world.

About Nicki

Nicki Gregory Koch grew up in the Panhandle of Texas, began her real estate career as an investor in 2005 and became a licensed agent in 2011. After being an investor during the '08 and '09 crash, she wanted to help others avoid real estate pitfalls. Since then, she has managed over $60 million in transactions and has worked in residential, commercial, investment, and farm and ranch. Nicki is a Certified Mentor and a certified eXpress Offers Agent with eXp Realty and is also a Certified Home Buyers Agent and Home Sellers Agent with the National Association of Expert Advisors.

There isn't much she hasn't had an opportunity to experience in real estate over all these years. Now, she also specializes in helping other agents grow their businesses. Nicki attributes her success to having a positive mindset, an ability to adapt to any situation and/or challenge, and a love for problem solving. One of her favorite things to say is "Everything is figuroutable."

Nicki believes that we are given gifts and talents as real estate agents to not only help people with buying and selling homes, but also to serve a higher purpose. She is passionate about finding ways to help agents use their business as a platform to make the world a better place. This is what led her to become the founder of AgentsACT.com. Agents ACT – Agents Against Child Trafficking, is the first real estate-led initiative to fight child trafficking and is what drives her in everything else that she does.

Nicki and her husband James, also a licensed real estate agent, live in West Texas. They love traveling to the mountains, cooking, modern design, and working on their 60's home in the country. You will find them frequenting local antique stores or anywhere there is great food. Nicki and James also love spending time with their four kids and dogs and running their multiple businesses.

For anything else you want to know about Nicki, go to:

- www.NickiGregory.expert

CHAPTER 10

THE SEVEN BABY STEPS TO PRODUCTIVITY

BY PHIL STRINGER

Becoming a six-figure agent isn't rocket science. It's not based on luck, and it's not even based on skill.

Unfortunately, many skilled sales professionals have been set up perfectly for success but failed at Real Estate because they never mastered the basics of productivity. Instead, they focused on everything else but never learned how to consistently take control of their calendar, set appropriate goals, or prioritize tasks to get the right things done at the right time.

Showing up without a clearly defined plan is a massive waste of time, and you'll think at the end of the day, "What did I do to advance my business today? I feel like I didn't move the needle at all."

YOUR DRIVING FORCE: A SYSTEM

Real Estate is a contact sport. The more contacts you make, the more successful you'll be. Your sphere of influence will only continue to grow as you consistently put in the work to make as many contacts as you can. Over time you will establish your authority and expertise in the market, and you'll become top of mind when people are ready to buy or sell. The key is to stay in front of them consistently, so that when they are prepared to move (whether next month, next year, or in 5 years), you're the one they think about when they think: "...Oh, we need a Real Estate agent. Let's call them!"

If you don't learn how to leverage your time and create scalable, repeatable processes, you'll always hit a ceiling, and eventually, you'll burn out before achieving your goals. Unfortunately, too many agents try to master the art of lead generation, advertising, marketing, systems, applications, and automation before they ever master the essential habits needed to succeed.

Using my 'Seven Baby Steps to Productivity' the basics of productivity can be unlocked. The door to success in your Real Estate business will swing open for you; you'll skip past the common pitfalls.

PHIL STRINGER'S SEVEN BABY STEPS TO PRODUCTIVITY

Let's face it. Many professionals get into Real Estate to avoid structure. They want to be their own boss. They want to escape the 9-5. However, most agents get their license, go out, then flop out. They made the ultimate mistake; they tried to avoid structure when, really, structure was the very thing they needed to become successful.

That fact changes today with my *Seven Baby Steps*:

Step (1) Create an External Brain:

- "I need to remember to call and set up a home inspection tomorrow."
- "I need to remember to clean the car."

- "I need to call and set up the photography for 123 Main St."
- "I need to run a CMA in Ms. Smith's neighborhood."
- "Oh, we're out of milk; I need to remember to run by the store after work."
- "I need to sign up for that new training."
- "I need to call my parents."
- "I have a PTA meeting this week."

Close the book and try and repeat all the points here – you probably won't remember every detail. It's true in life as well; we can't remember everything.

To start, create your 'brain dump' – this is one centralized master task list where you 'dump' personal or business to-dos, essentially everything on your plate. It's the catch-all space you'll sort through later, the perfect place to dump your fresh ideas as they come to mind so you can keep your mind clear. Anything and everything; they all go into this list.

Personally, I only have two sections, business and personal. Everything falls into one of those two categories. We'll organize it further in one of the next steps, but dump everything into this list for now. You'll immediately feel a sense of cognitive relief knowing everything is out of your mind and into a trusted source.

As a Real Estate agent, it's essential to also select a CRM for client data and dump every lead you have in this system. Some agents only use an Excel spreadsheet, and some use a specific CRM database, but either way, you should have all leads in only one place. All lead contact information should be compiled from the notes in your phone, address book, sticky notes, and any emails or messages, and dumped into the CRM of your choice. I personally use one system for my task list and another system strictly for Real Estate lead contact information.

Take a sigh of relief. You've now started the journey of becoming organized and intentional.

Step (2) Define Your Focus:

Often we misinterpret the meaning of 'focus'. We think of focus as the art of determining what to commit to. In reality, focus is the art of knowing what to ignore. It's what you say no to. Your focus can be found through distilling a few unique personal values and knowing them well.

Core Values

If we don't define our 'why', we will naturally end up just doing what we want, not what drives us toward our mission. That's where we think at the end of the day: "I feel like I didn't do anything worthwhile today." But, honestly, you probably didn't if there wasn't a clearly stated mission to accomplish.

Set 3-5 personal core values. Whether you're a solo agent or running a team of 100, you must have core values set for your business. Think about things that are personal values that drive you. Set no less than three and no more than five. Just as in your personal life, your core values act as a filter for everything in your business, including hiring, firing, the type of business you take on, and the way you expand; they show who you are and what you stand for.

Sometimes it's easier to list several values, then cut the number back. Just make sure you keep it simple and easy to remember. Each core value should only be between one and five words each. You might be wondering, is this who I am, who I want to be, or who I want to be seen as? In a perfect world, your core values will touch some of all three.

Mission Statement

Mission statements aren't easy, but they are crucial to define. Don't get too fancy here; keep it clear, simple, and easy to remember. Why did you choose to get into Real Estate? What is your passion? This mission statement should give you a sense of purpose, help guide your decision-making, and inspire you. Maybe your passion is to help first-time home buyers achieve the American dream. Maybe your passion is to help fight discrimination and ensure equal housing opportunities.

Whatever it may be, your mission statement should represent what you do and why you do it. It should come from the heart.

This is your why.

Step (3) Set a Strategic Plan:

This is where you start to develop real momentum. No more guessing; you know where you're headed; this is like determining an address to put into your GPS. Now each assigned task is like a step in the navigation that will move you closer to your destination.

- *Set your 10-year target first.* Determine what metrics matter to you – maybe it's the number of homes sold, a certain income/commission level, total revenue generated, the number of clients served, the number of people on your team, or total profit generated. Where do you want to be ten years from now? What metrics would you be thrilled to achieve? Be sure they are objectively measurable, no matter what metrics you choose.
- *Set your 3-year target based on your 10-year target.* To hit your 10-year target, where do you need to be in those same measurables to be on track to hit the 10-year goal?
- *Set your 1-year target based on your 3-year target.* To hit your 3-year target, where do you need to be in those same measurables to be on track to hit the 3-year goal?

Above all, set targets with specific and measurable metrics.

Step (4) Set Your Quarterly Goals:

A goal without a plan is just a wish. So now that you have a 10-year target broken down into a 1-year target, we have to create a plan to achieve that 1-year goal. This is where we determine what 3-7 things must be done in the next 90 days to be on track to hit your 1-year target.

What are the most important things that could be accomplished in the next 90 days to move the needle the most in your life and business? Set no less than three and no more than seven. Your focus for the next 90 days will be on these 3-7 goals.

Every 90 days, you'll assess where you are in relation to your 1-year goal. Didn't make the progress you thought during Q1? Time to bump up the effort and make up for it in Q2. Met your goal? Then it may be time to shoot higher and set loftier goals for the next quarter.

Step (5) Create Your Weekly Plan:

The number one reason why people abandon their task list (Brain Dump) is that they become so overwhelmed with the number of things to do that they eventually won't even return to their brain dump to add new action items to it or to use it to determine what needs to get done.

So, what's the solution?

A weekly planning session.

1) Pick a day of the week, Sunday being the most obvious for those with a Monday-Friday work schedule, to set your weekly plan, using your brain dump master list as the 'bank' to pull from.
2) Select everything that must be done or that you would like to complete in the coming week. Then, move these items to a completely separate list called 'This Week'. Now you have a shorter, more manageable list to work from – without all the overwhelm of a brain dump.

Always remember to keep your lists separate:

- Your brain dump is for making sure nothing is forgotten

and for referencing only once a week during your weekly planning session, but it is not to be used actively during your workday.

- Your weekly list is for actionable items that can be finished within the timeframe of your week. This is the task list you will actively work from each day.

The weekly tasks you've selected should include whatever is necessary to progress on the 3-7 quarterly goals you've set and anything you need to accomplish in daily life; in a way, it is your guide for navigating a busy week. Sometimes tasks will pop into your mind during the week, and if it's something that has to be completed that week, add it to your weekly list. If not, throw it in the brain dump for sorting later.

Step (6) Create Your Daily Plan:

Now you've filtered a 10-year target down to the things you need to focus on this week. You have a clear path to what needs to be done, and you've eliminated the overwhelm of everything else on your plate. It's time to get to work.

Your daily plan will include a morning startup and an evening shutdown routine. Every day during your evening shutdown, you'll select the three most important things that must be done the following day.

Refer to your 'This Week' list and decide which three items will be tagged as 'Today' for the following day. If you finish all three and still have time during the workday, add the next most important thing from the 'This Week' list and continue working until you run out of time.

If you don't complete all three 'Today' items in the workday, then shift the remaining incomplete items to tomorrow, and add however many new tasks needed to get the number back to three for the following day.

Implementing these two routines will be a significant benefit to helping you stay on track and to reduce cognitive stress.

Morning Startup
Before you start your workday, take the first 15-30 minutes and schedule an event on your calendar called 'Morning Startup'. This time is used for reviewing the three things you've tagged as 'Today' from the evening before, reviewing events on your calendar, and confirming or editing your time blocks to ensure your calendar is set for the day ahead. (More on this in Baby Step 7.)

Evening Shutdown
At the end of your workday, take the last 15-30 minutes and schedule an event on your calendar called 'Evening Shutdown'. This is when you review your 'This Week' list and set the three most important 'Today' items to be completed the next day. Tie everything up, shut everything down.

Now you're set and ready to start out of the gate when you have your 'Morning Startup" the next day.

Step (7) Time Block:

Just like giving every dollar a job in a financial budget, this is a budget for your time. Give every minute a job. Block out times for meetings, times for calling prospects, times to respond to messages, and times for training and development. Every minute should be given a name, even if that name is 'lunch'.

Your time block includes your three 'Today' items, which is based on your weekly plan, which is based on your quarterly goals, which is based on your 1-year target, which is based on your 3-year target, which is based on your 10-year target.

You must give every minute a job, or else you'll react to events happening around you, not proactively work on tasks that will drive you to success. When you do, you'll find the strength and willpower to get things done.

That all sounds great in theory, but guess what? You'll never have a perfect day.

IT'S ALL ABOUT FLOW

Let's face it, the time you block ahead of time will not always be how you spend your day.

Learning how to edit your time block is essential when reacting to challenges – when 'things come up'. When this happens, it is crucial to know how to rebuild your time for the day to accommodate the new challenge – the original time block you set isn't going to be perfect.

Most days, I have to reschedule my time block at least once or twice, but that's ok because a time block is just a guide meant to be fluid. Being intentional will pave the way to accomplishing your goals. Perfection is a disguise for inaction, and inaction is the enemy of productivity.

You Know the Seven Baby Steps… Now Use Them!

Imagine if you knew your goals ahead of time at pivotal moments in your life:

- How far could you go if you always had the space to act according to your core values?
- If your attention was always 'on point'?
- If you were always focused?

Straight to success in the form you're looking for, I would say. If you implement these baby steps in order, you will be productive in whatever you do, in your profession, Real Estate or not, and in life in general – friendships, relationships, and beyond.

About Phil

Phil Stringer's career started when he moved to Greensboro, North Carolina at a young age. He founded one of the first online arbitrage businesses, buying and selling products through a worldwide network he created. By the time he was 17 years old, he was generating six figures with what he learned online and taught himself about sales and marketing.

At 18, Phil Stringer started his formal sales career with General Electric. He was named the Top Sales Agent worldwide by the end of his first full year with the company, with a closing rate 1,180% higher than the average agent.

Over the last 15 years since attaining that success, Phil has honed his sales, team building, coaching, and business skills, being hired as the Chief Operating Officer at one of North Carolina's most successful real estate brokerages. In addition to his responsibilities with the company, Phil coaches agents, helping them to achieve their goals and dreams by not just becoming better salespeople, but also improving their quality of life through strategic planning, systems, processes, lead generation, social media coaching, time management, and mindset management in addition to his *Seven Steps*.

Most recently, Phil has created a study program called "How Do I Pass?" that helps North Carolina real estate students pass the national and state exam easily on the first try. By helping agents succeed so early in their careers, Phil has created a great network of agents to coach and support; this system has begun to expand, with real estate schools all over the country looking to partner with his brand.

Jay Kinder, Top 10 Revenue Share Earner at eXp Realty, and Former #2 Agent Worldwide at Coldwell Banker, had this to say of him:

"Phil exploded onto the real estate scene and quickly established himself as one of the most influential resources in the game. He possesses the vision and skills needed to take agents to the next level. If you're looking to drastically improve your business, you need to find a way to get in the same room as Phil Stringer."

Cliff Freeman, Top 5 revenue share earner worldwide at eXp Realty, and top DFW Realtor with 35 years' experience said this about Phil:

"Phil Stringer is on a mission to change lives and help fellow real estate practitioners become all that they can be. Well on his way to putting his dent in the universe, take heed: Phil will either see you at the top or from the top!"

Phil also has a passion for music. He loves singing and performing, which has been a creative outlet for him since he was young. Singing and leading worship at his local church is one of the things he cherishes most, but his greatest joy is being a father to his three kids, Nora, Hudson, and Mila.

Phil can be found via his website where he offers consulting, amongst other services, helping agents and professionals reach new heights they've only dreamed of.

Phil's website:

- www.philstringer.com

CHAPTER 11

THE REALITY OF REAL ESTATE

BY JAMES (JIM) McCLAIN

I've coached many agents for many companies, most recently with EXP Realty, but no matter where I've gone, or what agents I've taught, there is always a basic question that any and every agent looking to grow will ask:

"What am I supposed to do to grow my business?"

I've been in the real estate business since 1980, when interest rates went as high as 22%, and have learned a lot in these thirty, going on forty years, but the basic ideas never change. The answers have always been simple, but difficult to nail down.

Until now.

Step One: Have A Goal

Above and beyond anything else, you have to have a goal. Don't read another line here until you have a goal written down.

You can want a hundred thousand dollars, or you can want a million dollars, but unless you put it in writing, it is nothing but a dream. If you're embarrassed to put your idea on paper, you aren't ready yet. Come back when you are.

Step Two: Be Ready to Stretch Yourself

You have your goal down? If not, come back once you have something on paper. If so, great.

So do you want to gross a hundred thousand, or do you want to net a hundred thousand? I would say net; taxes are going to take a chunk out. In that regard, you'll have to do 30-40% above your goal in order to meet it, taking out responsibilities.

"How many do I have to do every month to attain a hundred thousand dollars net, figuring I can land a few deals with every set of potential clients?"

If you're new and have a lot to learn, or worse, no good at what you do, you're going to have to talk to maybe fifty potential clients to find one. Giving clients the time they deserve, at maximum, you can fit five in during the course of an eight-hour day. That's a month's worth of work for one potential commission.

Not effective! It's going to take two appointments to get one sale.

Step Three: Your Customers are KING and QUEEN

My whole thing has always been 'WOW' service, just as if I worked in a store or restaurant – I want my tips.

If you, as a customer, like you, you're going to send referrals because when their friend or family member talks about real estate, they're going to say, "Hey, my guy or my lady did this for me. You need to talk to them – I'm sure they can do it for you!" That could be thousands of dollars in your pocket without much work.

On the other side of that coin, are you going to have days that aren't productive? Absolutely, you're going to have that, but you also have to look at it that everybody has those days, and you cannot let that consume your thoughts.

Step Four: Know Who You're Serving

The harsh truth is that you will have to find new business consistently each and every day, each and every year. If your Rolodex isn't constantly expanding, your income potential will start to gather dust with it.

I've seen that many new agents worship the goal; they imagine what they'll do with the money they'll make – and that's an instant setup for failure. The truth is that the aim can never be about your commission. It has to be about your clients' wants and needs. When you meet those conditions, you make your commission. It isn't a formula; it is about human connections and understanding.

You cannot do and dream about this business 24/7. It will burn you out.

Step Five: Always Return the Favor

You bend over backward for your clients for each sale, and that's true – remember to reward yourself for a job well done; that's part of your duties as an agent, taking care of yourself. With each step toward your goal, aka, completing a sale, reward yourself sensibly. Go out to dinner, buy a new piece of sporting equipment, or go out for the evening. Do something that makes you feel alive.

It's just like flying an airplane. You do not leave Reagan airport in DC and go straight to Las Vegas along the same path you started on. Wind currents will buffet the plane and change its course in ways you can't control, no matter what.

Step Six: Find What Makes You Unique

What's your USP? Your 'unique selling point'.
- What would you do?
- What can you do?

You're in competition with hundreds of other agents, many much more seasoned, connected, better Rolodexes, or entire teams of staff. Why pick you?

To find your own unique selling proposition, I have a few steps to follow, as I teach in coaching sessions:

1. What do my customers want?
   - What are my customers truly looking for beyond selling or buying a home?
   - What kind of interactions are my customers looking for?
   - How can I deliver on my customers' expectations realistically while opening myself to minimal risk?

2. What are my personal values?
   - Writing them down, what are my top ten personal values in life?
   - From these ten personal values, what five of these hold up my business philosophy?
   - How do my personal values affect my business?

3. What are my strengths?
   - Taking my personal values into account, what are my strengths? List out ten of them.
   - From the ten strengths I have, which five can I immediately put into practice?

4. How do I translate my strengths into a unique selling proposition (USP)?

As the old saying goes, "you've gotta' have a gimmick." —

"I guarantee to sell your home at a price acceptable to you, or I'll buy it now." This is my own personal USP. That's one hell of an incentive, with the smaller print of 'terms and conditions apply.' The condition is that I have to see the home and value it ahead of time. I can quickly, usually within a day or two, find myself with a potential client in a sacred space, their home, making a personal connection.

If they don't like you and don't trust you, you're dead in the water. It's the same idea as meeting a potential surgeon. You wouldn't want somebody who got a 'D' in medical school doing your heart surgery, even if it was an emergency, most of the time. At least, I personally wouldn't. Picking a home is a life-altering decision with few ways to back out once it is finalized. It is a tricky subject.

My USP is a security blanket. "Well, if I end up not liking the house, at least he'll help me." It is a two-for-one. A client can be helped out of the home they wish to sell, then, if they dislike the new home over time, I already have a connection to help them leave to find another home. Two for the price of one, at least.

Step Seven: Learn 'No'

The word 'no' isn't your enemy – in fact, it is a green flag. "No," translated, says "I don't have enough information yet to make a commitment."

Step Eight: Social Media; It Isn't Optional

When you're prospecting, whether you're doing social media, direct mail pieces, or just phone call prospecting, have a reasonable goal and a set timeframe to do the work each day. We know that, but there's another truth lumped in with this step – knowing that social media and networking are a necessity, not an option.

I'll give you a forgotten tip, though, a tool to put back in your kit, circle prospecting. Search for homes just sold in your area, find the neighbors, and start dialing. "I just wanted to give you a heads up that your neighbors down the street at 123 Anywhere St. just sold their home for above asking price. Your neighborhood is pretty hot. Do you know what your home is potentially worth?"

It doesn't matter what company sold it, it's not what you're saying, but you are circle prospecting to let them know that this is what it's sold for and, more importantly, making that connection. "Do you want to talk more about your own home and your goals for your next move? So that we can get you top dollar in your timeframe with the least problems?"

The key word is to be reasonable. We work in a business where we are sometimes forced to tell clients this when it comes to expectations and budgets, but where is the bar set for us as agents? I can tell you where and why we aren't taught it in real estate school; it is all personal.

Find yourself an accountability partner, someone that you can roleplay your scripts with; practice, practice, practice – be ready to set boundaries, have conversations, and keep the process moving. These practices will make sure clients will want to work with you as opposed to anyone else in this business – they'll know that you know your stuff and that they can trust you.

You know, someone once told me it's not the best realtor that makes the money. It's the best marketer. It's the best conversationalist. And it's true. Don't think of yourself as a marketer? Refer to the following steps.

Step Nine: It's All About Relationships

Contact is what drives business. You are dealing with a human necessity. You have to have somewhere to live, a roof over your head. As an example, I had a sales agent making calls, earning a commission on the sales, which he helped to kickstart by making an introduction.

As he's going through his series of questions, all of a sudden, he hears a dog barking in the background and asks about what kind of dog it is – all of a sudden, he's on the phone with her for 20 minutes talking about the dog. He didn't get the appointment and didn't get anything else from her. My question to him was simple. "What did you accomplish?"

His answer was simple, too…"Nothing."

"You didn't accomplish anything because you didn't find out what her motivation was. Much less what her timing was; what if she doesn't want to move for three years? You can break that in half. You can probably drive that down to a year or at least make her start thinking about it."

You also must nurture these leads while facing the hard truth; they're not all going to be 'now' business, but statistics work in our favor in multiple aspects – for one, repeat calls over time create neural pathways that create a memory around your name. Second, statistically, human beings are creatures that like to move – it is in our DNA, roving around, moving away from predators.

"How long have you lived where you lived? Five years? Wow. Let me ask, if you ever decided to sell, where would you like to move to?" By asking these questions to 'no' prospects, you're setting up a timeline. Call them back in a few months. "By the way, have your plans changed at all? Are you still a year out, or are you looking to possibly do something sooner?"

Now, suddenly, again, you are engaging them, plus you're giving them an escape valve to make a decision. This is your chance to open that steam escape wider – maybe to remind them what the current marketability of their house is, that you'll offer to buy it, or if one of their neighbors sold a home for a good price. You're performing all of the functions of a friend looking to help.

Step Ten: Always Keep Your Word

MIT conducted a study that confirmed what we all know—callback times are one of, if not the most important factor, in securing business. Why? We all want to feel important, cared about, and listened to. The difference is five minutes.

Calling back within thirty minutes is a hundred-fold difference. That's a full 100% difference between five and thirty minutes. Makes you want to pick up the phone, right? You have competition every day in this. That article is free, and other agents know about it – I even teach this point in my own coaching seminars.

70-75% of leads are never called back, and half of them are called back within 24 hours. In this market, these leads might as well be kissed goodbye. As agents, we have to keep our word; callbacks and met appointments make up the rocket fuel that can shoot us to the moon or blow out our engine before liftoff if we're on empty.

Step Eleven: Tell the Truth

If you don't have an answer to something, don't fake it. "You know, that's a very good question. I don't have that answer right now but let me jot that down, and I'll call you back. Is that okay?" That's the best response you could give. They're not going to say no.

Again, you are building rapport – after all, you're working for them without complaint, and you're making and meeting promises, all of which are the baseline for a great working relationship.

Step Twelve: Most Importantly, You Aren't Alone

The key is consistency. You can't call today and never call again for the next three or four weeks. How would that make someone feel? Multiply that out for many clients, plus potential clients, and that's twenty or thirty calls a day as you grow your book of business. Impossible!

Now, once you get to a certain point, now you start delegating, right? …perhaps a virtual assistant, an inside sales agent. No matter what avenue you choose, there's work to give out. Pay someone to make those calls for you. Sure, it may cost $2,500 monthly with commissions and bonuses; however, with even five to ten transactions coming in per month, the costs are greatly offset.

$50,000 per month in exchange for $5,000 in payments? Absolutely.

After all, clients pay us for our knowledge; they pay us for our expertise. They pay us to make sure that we get them top dollar for their house with the least number of problems and in their timeframe, not to sit around and dial up other prospects, ignoring their needs. I need someone else to be doing that for me.

All this employee has to do is use the criteria and set the appointment. I'll take care of the rest when I get there. Because again, when you get there, it's the same scenario.

"What can I help you with?"

Step Thirteen: Remember the Reason

You are never tied to the outcome of a call; you're tied to the action taken after it ends.

About James

James McClain Sr., known by clients, family, and friends as Jim, entered into the real estate industry in 1980 when interest rates were 16 to 22% – a time when it seemed like the real estate market was headed for an immediate crash and new agents could be eaten alive by the 'bigger fish' in the 'small pond' that was real estate anywhere in the U.S.

Despite tall odds, Jim knew his USP, his unique selling proposition, and was able to put together a book of business that would serve as the concrete foundation for the start of his career.

In his words, "I was fortunate enough to help 55 families my first year just by understanding that it was a human interaction; when people are making such a huge, dedicated commitment, they want personalized service and attention – they have to be able to trust you as a person, or you'll never make a sale. Since I understand that, I have been a top multimillion-dollar producer for all 42 years I've been in the business."

Jim has enjoyed the opportunity to play coach and leader of The Success Series at the Fredericksburg Area Real Estate Association Board and mentor countless agents for EXP Realty, having gained his experience in the school of 'hard knocks' in his 42 years of service, including opening and operating his own realty company, Greater Virginia Realty, up until the crash in 2008.

"I love giving back, helping agents to achieve their highest-possible success, no matter what company they work for. We all have something that we can learn from each other, no matter what. That's one of the best perks in this business – we're always learning something. Every agent in the area knows they can call me; I'm always answering questions."

Hands down, the biggest question Jim gets from new and seasoned agents alike circulates around one central idea: "What's my USP?"

Jim has an honest answer: *"Your USP is what makes you unique and how you can use that unique element of your personality to make a sale. We all have one main USP and a few backups. Finding your USP has become a major part of any consultations or training that I do. Finding it is almost a lost art—and if you look around, the top-selling agents out there know and exploit theirs."*

In his free time, Jim enjoys playing poker and spending time with his family.

To send Jim a message or book him for a training session, you can reach him by phone at:

- (540) 846-7400.

CHAPTER 12

66,795
HOW INCREMENTAL IMPROVEMENT CHANGED MY HEALTH, MY RELATIONSHIPS, AND MY CAREER!

BY SAM BASEL

The word 'restless' resonated deeply within me. I knew I needed a change, but I didn't know what that change was. From the outside looking in, everything in my life appeared fine, but I wasn't satisfied. I had a successful business, but I wasn't excited about my role as it was. I had a strong relationship with my wife and my kids, but I worried whether I was around enough to be the husband and father they needed me to be. I lived in the mountains of Colorado, but I always dreamed of having more time for adventures.

It seemed all aspects of my life demanded more of me than I had to give. Something was stirring inside me and I couldn't solve it. In a word, I was stuck...but I wasn't giving up.

On New Year's Eve, I decided to make a resolution. It wasn't as much a resolution as it was a decision to *take action* on something I could control. My goal was to begin an exercise program doing sit-ups and push-ups starting with doing one of each on January 1st and then add one more sit up and one more push-up each day for the entire year. To make things more interesting starting out, I also decided to run for 30 minutes each day and track my progress. I was excited about a program that was simple and didn't require any special equipment besides my running shoes and my treadmill if necessary. The reps I needed to do each day correlated to the number of days that had passed on the calendar in a year, so it was easy to keep on track with that as well.

I did the math and I'm not going to lie...the result scared me quite a bit! If I accomplished my goal of adding one more each day, that means I would be committing to 66,795 push-ups, and 66,795 sit-ups in one year's time, not to mention the 182 hours, 30 minutes of running that I would have to do. I wondered if I had the mental toughness to complete the task for all 365 days. The more I thought about the big goal, the more impossible it seemed to accomplish. However, by focusing on how easy it was to do just one push-up and one sit-up, it also seemed ridiculously easy to get started. By breaking the big goal down into *small, simple tasks*, the goal seemed much more achievable.

Having been involved in sports and being reasonably athletic most of my life, I didn't find the push-ups or sit-ups difficult to start and didn't take much time to finish. As I started out early in the year, I wondered when it would get difficult or when life would get in the way and force me to stop for some reason. As I passed 50 push-ups and then 75, I started breaking up the number of push-ups into equal sets to make up my total for the day. I also alternated from sit-ups to push-ups and back again until I reached my total I was shooting for each day. About the time I started hitting 3 sets of 50, I started to believe this whole thing was actually possible.

The monotony involved doing push-up after push-up was a mental roadblock as much as it was a physical one. There were days I didn't feel like getting out of bed and dedicating the time necessary to accomplish that day's goals. There were some days where I was running and exercising late into the night just to get back up in the early morning to do it all over again. Eventually, the amount of time it took to accomplish each set of exercises and the rest needed in between sets took longer than it did to run for 30 minutes. I had no choice but to **be intentional with my schedule** to fit it all in with the rest of my schedule for the day.

My four kids and my wife were a huge support through the entire process sometimes joining in to see how many they could do alongside of me. Everyone in my family knew my goal and that helped me stay accountable. They knew I had to make time to get it done, and over time I began to want to accomplish this goal to show my kids what was possible. I didn't want to let them down. At times, they didn't know how to encourage me to keep pushing until the concept of improving 'one more than yesterday' came into our discussions. From then on, all I focused on was 'one more than yesterday.'

After a while, the threat of breaking the streak seemed like a bigger disappointment than how easy it was to just add one more. The days turned into weeks which turned into months… and eventually, the end of the year and the end of the program came into focus. I'm proud to say I accomplished my goal without skipping a single day all year long! While each day was hard, the crazy thing was that over time, my body and my mindset got used to the hard work. Somewhere along the line, the hard work turned into 'business as usual' through focusing on **'one more than yesterday'** and staying disciplined to the process.

If you thought that was the end to my story, I'm excited to share it was only the beginning!

Before I finished all 365 days, my mindset and my goals for everything else I wanted to accomplish in my life began to expand exponentially. When I started out, each day was difficult and took effort. As I added incrementally more exercise each day and ran faster on my treadmill, what seemed hard at the beginning became easy by the end of the year. It took me a while, but I learned that growth takes time!

At this point in our lives, our kids were growing like crazy and instead of leaning heavily into my career with my new-found direction, I chose to press pause to pursue time with my family. I set a goal to step out of my business for three months to travel the country in an RV with my family. At first, this goal seemed just as daunting as all those push-ups and sit-ups. But I also had the new confidence that I could figure out the steps necessary, make it a priority, and get it done.

Much like the exercise plan, I focused on the small steps it took to accomplish the goal and knocked them out one step at a time. Being complete novices in the recreational vehicle department, we did a bunch of research, purchased the RV, set up the company to operate while I was on the road, and took off on a trip of a lifetime! We saw all 48 states in three months as a family, made countless memories, and invested in our relationships. Living as a family of six in 350 square feet for three months will make any family closer, and we wouldn't trade it for the world! While I could easily go down the rabbit hole of all the amazing things we saw, the routes we took, and the people we visited, the point is: WE DID IT! We had the time of our lives!

When I returned home, I was thrilled to see that my business not only survived but was just as healthy as when I left thanks to my amazing employees and colleagues. The idea that I could leave for three months and still have a thriving business opened a whole new world of possibilities in my mind and in my career. Much like the exercise program, and the RV trip after it, I was dreaming big dreams again with the confidence I could figure out the steps necessary, and get it done!

The process of focusing on myself ended up **benefiting everyone around me**. Specifically, my family benefited not only from the big RV trip that brought us much closer as a family, but they also saw an example of how to set big goals, make a plan, have the discipline to stick to the plan, and come out successful on the other side. My co-workers and employees benefited from me having a bigger vision for my company and the opportunities that have come along with that vision. My clients benefited from my positive attitude and willingness to tackle big problems to find solutions.

In a world that always seemed to demand more of me than I had to give, I enjoyed making myself and my health a priority. Conquering the mental side of the exercise program allowed me to think bigger and gain self-confidence that I didn't know I had lost. Through the discipline of 365 days of exercise, I broke out of my restlessness and found my way from being stuck to being unstuck.

APPLICATION TO REAL ESTATE

By this time, you may be wondering how my story of 66,795 push-ups and sit-ups will help you learn how to make your first $100,000 in real estate. Let's look back again at a few of the key lessons from my story and consider how they can be applied to being a successful real estate agent.

Key Lesson #1: Take Action

You never know what you can accomplish until you **take action**. By focusing on your own effort and what you can control, you'll achieve success faster. In the world of real estate, it seems as if there are a lot of things outside of your control before you receive a paycheck. But what you can control is your own effort. You can't control other people's decisions, but you can control how many people you connect with in a day. Taking that first step is the hardest part, but it may also be the most important! Take action on things you can control, and let the results take care of themselves.

Key Lesson #2: Small, Simple Tasks

Big goals are easier to accomplish when you break them down into **small, simple tasks**. Break your big goals down into tiny steps that build off the previous steps. Eventually, what you found hard to accomplish yesterday becomes easier if you stay disciplined to the process. Small progress adds up to massive gains over time.

Key Lesson #3: Be intentional with your schedule

Being intentional with my schedule was essential to structure my day to include what I decided was important in my life. "Not having time" is just an excuse. If it is important enough, you'll make time. Start first by planning time for yourself, your family, and other things that bring you joy. Likewise, identify what in your real estate business that you absolutely need to be doing each and every day. Make sure you plan your day and your week so that you are focused on accomplishing those goals with time for your health, your finances, and your relationships. Use your calendar and technology to your advantage with timers, alerts, and alarms to keep yourself on track. It seems counterintuitive, but the more disciplined you are with your time, the more free time you will have to do things you want to do!

Key Lesson #4: Be Accountable to Someone

Having a group of people who supported my goals and **held me accountable** was necessary to get me through the tough times. Likewise, in real estate, the people you have around you are essential to your success. If the people around you don't inspire you to be better, dream big, and live out your unique abilities, then do everything you need to do to find your people! Seek out people that are a little bit ahead of you, a little bit behind you, and that are walking right alongside of you to get the most out of your relationships.

Key Lesson #5: Incremental Improvement

I found I could accomplish a lot more than I thought I could by simply adding **'one more than yesterday.'** Incremental progress in real estate doesn't have to be a daily thing but could be a weekly, monthly, or even yearly thing depending on your focus! It could easily look like adding one more person to your database, adding one more piece of marketing to your mix, contacting one more person, or one more closing. Be deliberate on what you can do that is just a little bit harder, a little bit faster, a little bit more than you did before. Your previous successes give you confidence to accomplish just a little bit more each time.

Key Lesson #6: Growth Takes Time

There was no way I could have done 66,795 push-ups and sit-ups in a short period of time. I had a hard time thinking 365 push-ups were even possible in a single day when I started the program. **Growth takes time**! Likewise, don't beat yourself up when you aren't selling 100's of houses each year as a rookie! Along these same lines, stop comparing your life to someone else's and never compare your beginning to someone's ending.

Key Lesson #7: Your Success Benefits Others

My attitude and mindset ended up **benefiting everyone around me**. In my story, my family, my clients, and my coworkers all benefited from my positive outlook on life and accomplishing my big goals. Remind yourself of who else would benefit from a successful career in real estate. Dream a little bigger with me here…how would the people around you benefit if you focused on incremental improvement to accomplish your big goals? What if you found $100,000 income to be easy? Better yet, what's stopping you from following all the great advice in this book and simply doubling the math?

The simple mantra of **'one more than yesterday'** allowed me to accomplish big goals, but also had a ripple effect that changed my life, my health, my relationships, my business, and my career. This story continues to change me to this day! My hope and prayer is that you find inspiration in my story to go out and change your life for the better by focusing on incremental improvement.

About Sam

Sam Basel is a family man and an entrepreneur who fell into real estate early in life. With a passion for helping others and looking out for their best interest, he has carved out a successful career in Estes Park, Colorado. He has been actively involved in the industry since 2004, growing throughout his career from a licensed personal assistant to a solo agent to a business owner and to a team leader through multiple real estate cycles.

Sam's journey in real estate began early on, and he quickly fell in love with connecting with people, solving real estate puzzles, and building wealth through real estate. Determined to fight against the poor public perception of real estate agents, he opened his own independent real estate agency in 2011. Alpine Legacy Real Estate was created with a focus on providing personalized service and working tirelessly to ensure that each of his clients' best interests were always at the forefront. Sam has represented clients in a variety of property types including primary homes, secondary homes, family legacy properties, investment properties, commercial properties, and properties in distressed situations.

Over the years, Sam's business has grown and flourished. He is now a respected team leader for the Alpine Legacy Team at eXp Realty, LLC, known for his expertise and focus on helping buyers and sellers make wise real estate decisions in any situation. He is also a passionate mentor and enjoys helping other agents build successful careers in the industry whether it be in Colorado or across the country.

In addition to his professional pursuits, Sam is a devoted family man who is married and has four children. He is actively involved in the ministry of Fellowship of Christian Athletes as a member of the Board of Directors for Northern Colorado and is deeply committed to serving his community. He also enjoys the outdoors, loves to travel, and is always seeking new experiences. He thrives on competition and is constantly setting and achieving new goals, both in his personal and professional life.

Overall, Sam Basel is a dedicated, hardworking, and well-rounded individual who is committed to helping others and is never afraid of taking on a challenge and accomplishing it with excellence. Whether it's in real estate or in his personal life, he's always looking to make a positive impact in any way possible.

Connect with Sam:

- AlpineLegacy.com
- SamBasel.com

CHAPTER 13

"WE ARE THE AUTHORS OF OUR OWN STORY."

BY CINDI FEATHERSTON-SHIELDS

I faced an upward climb entering the real estate business. I'm not from a wealthy family. I'm not from a family that believed in higher education. I didn't go to college. We were in survival mode as I was growing up and my parents will tell you that today. They were kids, raising kids and were very young when they had my brother and me. There were no big dreams of getting rich; the dream, quite simply, was to make sure the bills were paid and food was on the table.

My parents weren't from business backgrounds – my mom was a nurse, and probably expected I'd be a nurse, as well. Career assessments I completed in high school indicated that I'd be a nurse or a teacher. I thought I'd follow in Mom's footsteps, but I can't stand the sight of blood, even fake blood on TV, so that idea went straight out the window.

I remember telling my mom that I was going into real estate. The "Mhmm" she gave let me know she was listening, but she didn't put a lot of stock into what I was saying nor the way I felt. But I knew I wanted to do it and I would prove to her that

I could. Dad, like Mom, wasn't sure about it at first either. But he ended up supporting me, because there was a chance that I could pull it off and do something big. Now Dad calls and asks, "Did you make a million dollars today?" I always laugh him off, "Maybe not a million dollars, Dad, but I did pretty well." Their belief started building with each milestone I achieved, and I earned their support.

Today, I own an agency. And you can, too.

KNOW THIS BUSINESS IS A COMMITMENT

The dropout rate in real estate is extremely high, and it is easy to pinpoint the spot where the fallout happens. Taking classes, studying and passing the state and national exam, paying for a real estate license, getting established with a broker and the local, state, and national real estate associations is quite costly; it's easy for one's steam to vanish after all that money has been spent.

And while one perk of this business is having no boss (someone telling you to come in at a certain time, do a certain task, or act a certain way), this lack of structure, which may not be an issue for those who are committed, is likely to be a downfall for those who want only to 'put a toe in' and they are setting themselves up for a rough time, from the get-go.

FIND A MENTOR

I think it started when I graduated high school.

I met John, a guy 10 years older than me. He and his family were my first mentors; they were very successful, and I knew I liked that, even if I didn't know how to replicate it for myself. I liked what they were doing; I knew it was important to watch them and try to absorb as much information through osmosis as possible.

We're still friends to this day. We have coffee almost every morning after all these years. It's so good to have those people, lifelong friendships and mentors, people you know that you can still learn from no matter what, and the safety of knowing that someone has your back out there in this crazy world.

When I got into real estate, Annelle Harris was the first and only broker I worked for. She put me in the backseat of her Cadillac, and she drove me around, introducing me to people and taking me to luncheons, teaching me that the real estate business is about relationships, not numbers. I learned so much from her.

I've been mentored by our second longest-running sheriff in Texas, JB Smith, who taught me to find humor in situations and to relax and not take myself so seriously. And an attorney, David Dobbs, has taught me how to deal with people and think objectively. David encourages me to step out of my comfort zone on a regular basis.

It's a human business, not all about math, money, and statistics. You can learn from anyone – personal or business. It's important to follow opportunities to be around the right people, and never to aim to be the smartest person in the room. There's always someone better out there, so strive to be the best you can be.

Remember:

- Mentors are all around you; they aren't necessarily in your business or may not look like you – mentors are anyone you can learn from, a good influence who helps you to excel.
- Find many mentors who can teach you the ins, outs, and many angles. In real estate, you'll need someone to teach you the business, the math, the strategy, but also someone to coach you on the human relationship aspect – how to network, how to win over clients, even down to business etiquette and party planning.

- The key is to pick your strategy, learn how to improve it from mentors, and stick with it.

SET YOUR STRATEGY

So often, people pay for tons of training or bring in a consultant, but they never act. I coach people every morning and can tell who will act, and those who won't—they procrastinate or "need to do more research. It's like someone who wants to become a painter or a sculptor; it is important to know style and form to know how art works, but to be a great painter or sculptor, it will take years of hard work honing the physical ability to create art.

IT'S ALL ABOUT YOUR USP (UNIQUE SELLING PROPOSITION)

Time to ask yourself a few questions:

- Why should people want to work with me?
- What kind of relationships can I offer?
- When I start a relationship with a client, do I have a plan to continue it past the sale?
- How am I going to use my USP to 100%?

I can remember the defining moment when I found my USP set in stone; it was when we attempted to sell out the East Texas area's only residential high-rise. It was a battle against every other high-powered agent in the area, but units weren't selling as quickly as expected.

We took out billboards, ads, digital advertisements, and showed the units off on social media – we'd get a few calls here and there, we were selling units but not fast enough. I had to sit down and deeply think about moving the needle. My Coach, John Kitchens helped me with a strategy and held me accountable by checking in on me each week.

So, we did what other offices hadn't – we hired a chef whose explicit job was to help me host events and we fed people. Homeowners at the high-rise invited friends to visit, eat, and see what high-rise living is about. and it worked in a BIG way; many of those friends ended up being their neighbors!

These clients have become lifelong friends for me and my husband, Rob. They have watched our son Tony grow up while living in this beautiful high-rise. We eat dinner with them, celebrate birthdays with them, celebrate life with them, and even vacation with them. We've come to love them. Through time, we began to meet their friends, who became our clients, our sphere has grown through hosting events, playing golf, and being friends.

STICK TO YOUR USP

Some offices and agents buy Zillow or Realtor.com leads, which is part of their business model. Some run Facebook advertising. Some operate on word of mouth, and others operate on cold-calling or mailing potential customers based on sales statistics in certain neighborhoods. No matter what configuration, some offices succeed with these formats, but many do not. The question then becomes, for offices and agents that use a combination, but don't succeed, why do they frequently struggle to land clients? You probably already know the answer; it is because they are using a "scattershot solution" to find and retain clients rather than knowing and using their USP at 100% – they aren't doing what they do best.

Remember:

- 'When you love on people, the business builds itself.'
- When you use your USP at 100%, you set yourself up to use your sharpest tool effectively, giving you an edge over the competition.

IT'S ALL ABOUT MARKETING

Not just anyone can go to a cocktail party and work it like there's no tomorrow. I couldn't do that in the beginning. However, marketing 'thickens the gravy', as a cook would say. Let's face it, buying a property is a huge commitment, and for some buyers, it is one of the biggest investments they'll ever take on; a house can cost as much as someone will make through their entire career. Suffice it to say that your relationship should extend past the moment the commission check hits – after all, statistically, some buyers will purchase a second property or look to move within five years.

Within our office, it's all about relationships, and food is our primary way of nurturing those relationships. It's about delivering charcuterie boards and snack boxes to their doorstep. And not just sponsoring social events but providing beautiful food and hosting those events. Our goal is to be perfect neighbors; sending cards in the mail for birthdays and anniversaries, always giving, and always on call to lend a hand or have a quick chat.

Remember:

- Clients aren't a one-off; they are a relationship you'll need to carry – relationships are the fuel that drives business.
- Word-of-mouth marketing is the hidden supercharged jet fuel that can push you skyward. After all, if a friend or family member trusts you, it is likely that their friends or family will too.

ALWAYS BE CONSISTENT

Over 20 years ago, I became a broker and bought my real estate agency from my mentor, Annelle. I was in my twenties, the youngest person there. We went in to announce the sale, the ink still wet on the agreement papers, and when we did, seven of the thirteen agents walked out, never to be seen again.

My partner and I had just signed ourselves up for a hundred thousand dollars in debt. I had to make it work for those who stayed; there was no going back. I couldn't let myself, my partner, or my agents down – it was up to me to create an office that worked, drove income, and strived to be the best and that is what I did.

If you have that determination and drive, if somebody's invested time and money in you, you can't let them down. It keeps you accountable. Many agents don't get this; they lack the internal GRIT that says, "I have to succeed, to persevere, no matter how the deck is stacked."

It will be hard getting started, but the results, like anything in life that takes hard work, is worth it. It will pay for itself in the end when you taste success and see the effects—when you see that you've helped to change lives.

If you have the determination to go to real estate school, pass the tests, and join a brokerage, you have what it takes to make a change. Whether you are committed and or are "just sticking your toe in" can only be decided by you. Unless someone is paying your bills, you must do it. It is time to fly free.

Remember:

- Your name is only as good as your consistent track record – showing up to meetings on time, returning calls as soon as possible, and being available for clients professionally and personally.

YOUR MINDSET MATTERS

"Don't ever let them see dollar signs in your eyes because that's not what we're about. It's always about the people we serve." Those words from one of my mentors have stuck with me since they were said.

Why? Because it's true. Clients want to know that they're cared about, not just numbers on a spreadsheet tallying up commission checks.

Now more than ever, it's about people, the human connection, and showing the value you can bring clients while educating them; it's about giving them the care and respect we want.

YOU HAVE TO BE READY FOR THE CHANGE

When the mindset to succeed is there, you're automatically willing to take those next leaps, whether you doubt yourself or not. Being in the real estate business is a commitment to yourself, knowing that it will change your life for the better, but only if you put the work in to reap the reward.

WOMEN MATTER IN THIS BUSINESS

I truly believe a woman needs to know how to take care of herself, and she needs to know how to provide for herself and be able to provide for her family if necessary – partners get sick, they move on, and divorces happen.

Real estate is one of the few industries that a woman doesn't need a college education to enter; she can enter real estate and change her life, pulling her family into a better situation along with her in exchange for the hard work it takes to start.

Many women stay in relationships they might not, otherwise, if they don't know how to make money. They stay in terrible abusive relationships for money and/or stability, knowing that their family won't be hungry and homeless, even if home life isn't the best.

Remember:

- We only change when we're ready, not when other people

are ready for us. Change must come from inside when the time is right.

YOU CAN GO ANYWHERE

The real estate business is great and varied because it's not just about selling properties. You can be a real estate investor, a mentor and coach, or an agency owner. And a female in this business can do all kinds of things without fear of breaking a glass ceiling that so many other businesses have.

For women and men alike, there's unlimited potential for success in real estate; it is possible to change your circumstances and your LIFE through hard work.

About Cindi

Cindi Featherston-Shields is a highly accomplished and distinguished real estate professional – Committed! Determined! Experienced! These are just a few words that describe Cindi Featherston-Shields.

Cindi carries integrity, in-depth community and market knowledge, marketing savvy, effective negotiating skills, and access to a high-quality professional network—all the most crucial hallmarks of an effective collaborator and advocate for clients.

In her over 25 years as a top real estate professional in East Texas, she has found that to provide the very best service, it is essential to put her clients first. Cindi responds quickly to her clients' needs while maintaining accessibility and transparency throughout the buying and selling process.

Building relationships through a 'client first' philosophy has always been Cindi's approach and it requires her to continually improve her skills and keep pace with the latest technologies. This allows her to be more efficient while extending the range of services she provides her clients.

Cindi Featherston-Shields was voted Best of the Best Realtor by *BScene* magazine readers in 2006, 2008 and 2009, Top Real Estate Professional in East Texas, Local Love Us Realtor 2012 – 2018 and "Remarkable Women of East Texas." She was featured on the cover of *Real Producers of East Texas* in 2022 and ranked in the top 1% according to Realtrends.

Cindi is an active mentor in the real estate community and recently opened The Success Center, a full-service RE Agent Support Center for all. Cindi believes wholeheartedly in helping women to succeed in the real estate business. She knows it is one of the last industries where a woman can be inspired and empowered to pull herself out of challenging situations through hard work, education and resources.

When not pursuing real estate, Cindi serves as an outspoken and active advocate for animal welfare. She provides funding for the SPCA of East Texas with a boutique shop that she opened with other individuals just as passionate about improving the lives of animals.

Want to connect with Cindi? Get in touch with her through The Success Center at:

- www.SuccessCenter.vip

CHAPTER 14

REAL ESTATE MATCHMAKER

BY KRISTEN HAYNES

What I love about this business is its unlimited income growth and the opportunity for many different revenue streams. There is no ceiling! It is all driven by your determination, discipline, hustle and ability to add the right mentors that can fast-track your success!

I built my extremely successful business around the values of fairness, respect and doing what is right. In life, you're always choosing between right and wrong and I've always followed The Golden Rule. Not everyone will understand your dreams, so it is important to align yourself with those that do and make them a part of your success story.

I'm going to give you the keys to successfully creating a 100% Referral-Based or Sphere Business that is fun and never stops—this is how I quickly became a six-figure agent. I will provide you with my advice on how I manage work life balance, scaling my business and how I have created a business where I don't have to always compete for listings and buyers, but where people often know they want to work with me even before they have officially met me.

I was often told in the early years after college by friends and family that I would be great at and really love being a REALTOR®. I began my career in commercial banking for a national Bank and pursued this career for 8 years. During this period, my husband attended and graduated law school and we had our first daughter. Shortly after having our first daughter, I made the scary leap to the 100%-commission-and-no-benefits world of Real Estate sales (also after saving up for the possibility of having no income!). I joined a small 2-year-old local independent brokerage as a new agent and found myself often going to Google and books to seek out information on best practices and how to be successful as a REALTOR®. I had wonderful colleagues in the firm I looked to for advice and to whom I asked questions, but I knew I would have to look further outside of my bubble to become the next-level type of agent I wanted to be.

In my early days starting out as a Realtor, I would always try to make connections with real estate professionals around the country – authors of real estate books I liked and agents I admired and tried to learn from them. I attribute my work ethic, values and my ability to network and grow relationships as the drivers of my success. I wanted to be the agent with the best customer service and cutting-edge marketing tactics in our market. This lofty goal and strong determination kept me up late every night for many years seeking out the latest and greatest practices outside our local mid-sized market. I also spent time researching and implementing projects to grow my business.

Always exude passion and excitement for real estate, never negativity, advice that I share with each new agent I speak with today! I made it a priority to always answer or return calls as quickly as possible and made responsiveness one of my key values. One missed phone call or slow response could easily cost you a $10,000 client! Lastly, I made sure to be a resource to anyone for their real estate needs or questions – whether or not I got paid! Worst case it was a great learning opportunity, but oftentimes the person was so impressed or thankful that they shared my name with a potential client! These early strategies paid off, and I was consistently the top agent at the independent firm and consistently accounted for 10-15% of the annual firm sales for the last five years while working there.

In my years there, I had made my ambitions clear—achieving part ownership. In early 2020, my dream had come true! I was offered to buy out one of the partners nearing retirement. The details were to be hammered out, with a company evaluation to be completed after the tax deadline...and then the pandemic hit.

I waited patiently while tax deadlines were extended and I pushed through one of the most difficult times of my entire life - working full-time while having to homeschool two young children in a Spanish Immersion Program while caring for a toddler. These pressures were then intensified at the end of 2020 when I was given the blindsiding and devastating news that during that time I was patiently waiting and trying to hold life together, two of the three owners had negotiated the sale of their ownerships to a private equity investor. My dream was ripped away from me without so much as a courtesy discussion about how this would impact my future at the firm as the deal was being negotiated. I have always been one to fight for what is right and to be a strong advocate for my clients, family and friends, and now it was time to make the hard decision of adding yet another incredibly difficult thing to my plate. I just could not stay there any longer and had to leave what was comfortable for what was right. I was devastated.

After this setback, I put my head down, worked with the best marketing firm in town to create my new brand, and refined the vision, mission and values for my very own firm. Looking back, having the vision, mission and values were another driver of success. There is power behind a vision that you focus your actions and work toward. If you do not have these yet, even as a solo agent, you need to take the time to establish them. Build them into your everyday decision-making process!

I had been eyeing the eXp model for years, which is why it was a quick decision for me in aligning my vision and mission. It was the perfect turn-key solution and platform to run my own firm with the vision to be a local-impact-driven, collaborative firm with an excellent reputation to dominate my market with cutting-edge technology.

This move has turned out to be the best decision I've ever made professionally and is so fulfilling to be able to use my creativity how I want and focus on impacting the local community and my agents. I put myself 'in the room' with a huge network of agents who are levels above me, who are where I want to be, that are sharing their playbooks with me constantly. And I don't have to pay $1,000+ per month for it! In the first year with my new mentors, I saw my business grow by 60%!

Key focus areas in growing my business outside of the above-mentioned:

1. **Create Raving Fans:** I always go above and beyond even if there is no money to gain because it leads to future warm referrals of business. One raving fan client is worth far more than a handful or two of satisfied clients. The raving fans will advocate passionately for your business. Make your business one that is worth raving about; go beyond the call of duty! Show everyone how hard you work and how seriously you take the job. They will trust you more and be able to feel more comfortable giving your name to friends when they know that you are all-in on your client's success and happiness.

   Countless times I've seen my business multiply from certain ecstatic clients—that is something easy to quantify. Not everyone shares the name of their REALTOR® so you want to turn your clients into your business advocates. Communication and responsiveness can be key to this. And keep it personal. Do what it takes to make clients happy.

If there is a 'pothole' in the transaction, it's better to give $500 of your commission to make it smooth and gain future business than to dig your heels in on principle if it were out of your control. Even having to give up a little commission to come to terms on a deal, the repeat or referral business is worth so much more than that.

2. **Social Media and Creative Marketing:** I was an early adopter of social media and have been consistently told by clients and friends that it is a source of business – as they mention things they've seen me post when talking to me about their situation or referring me to others. I even have people I don't know (never worked with) who refer my name out. Even connections from the past who don't live in my city who refer me out because they see what I'm doing on social media. It works and I think that it is a 'must' to be successful in this day in age. It's so important to show your sphere and remind them of what you do, show your personality too! People work with people they know and trust. It's also just a free place to showcase examples of your sales and marketing to your sphere.

Our market is heavy on relocation, which was spurred by the pandemic in the past few years and now more companies and jobs are moving to our area. I've put more emphasis on targeting relocation buyers through social media including YouTube. My 'relocation' business prior to pandemic was about 15% 'relocation' and 85% local movers, while for the past few years it has been about 50% relocation, 15% investors, and 35% local movers. You want to think about making connections through social media with agents who may refer to your area often. Find realtors who you would mesh well with and who would likely have the type of clients like the ones you want to work with in cities that people often move from - follow and connect with them.

3. **Networking:** As I mentioned, my business is almost 100% referral or sphere based. As a real estate agent, every person you meet is a potential client. I am not a cold caller, so I chose to dive into my Sphere early on- it was fun! I would go to every young professional networking event that I could find. I joined Bunco groups, wine groups, book clubs, tennis teams, and threw 'welcome-to-the-neighborhood' parties. I embraced any opportunity to host that I could and always stayed connected with current friends while seeking to make new connections.

Another benefit of staying connected and in the community is keeping my antennae up for people selling or any opportunity for a client. I'm not always looking to list someone's house (which would be great too), I listen up for houses about to be sold to be a matchmaker for people buying or selling off-market. Nothing makes people happier than their agents making off-market magic happen. If you store enough people in your brain as 'possibly wanting to move' then you can sometimes find multiple transactions to make this happen for people. That is the magic. This has become one of my specialties—being able to find off-market properties—and it happens by being out and about within the neighborhoods you know and cherish. I've become the top-selling agent by volume in the neighborhood where I live and much of where my Sphere lives.

4. **Staying in Touch with Your Sphere Post-closing:** Past clients are the best source of future business; I think we've all heard this. I started with a monthly newsletter early on, created VIP Groups with events and where I shower them with gifts. I have developed an ambassador level of clients and contacts who send referrals on a regular basis. They are some raving fans and I frequently try to show my appreciation, whether it is a gift, a handwritten note, or a courtesy wine-tasting event. Always take note of their life events and reach out.

5. **<u>Leverage and Systems</u>:** In addition to the traditional way I started my business, I've become a big fan of leveraging my time and building best-practice systems and checklists. As you grow you should always consider a hire that can leverage your time to do more higher-income activities or those that you are best at. I first started with hiring a TC, then eventually added marketing help and a copywriter, a video editor, client care coordinator, an Operations Director to manage everyone, and now an SEO and website developer. The website developer is implementing my more advanced initiatives like becoming an unofficial 'neighborhood mayor' and then, our downsizing division.

It can be overwhelming to think about hiring someone, but you can start by doing a time inventory. You must delegate to achieve great success in this business and you can't become a six-figure agent while doing $25 per hour tasks. You will burn out.

6. **<u>Mentorship</u>:** I am a firm believer in having mentors to turn to for help so that you can go out and be confident in your abilities and win the business – if you aren't yet the expert then turn to your mentors for guidance. Confidence goes a long way in this business—it's hard to trust someone with such a large investment who doesn't exude confidence. So be confident! Win the business. Lean on a mentor that has a similar alignment of values.

7. **<u>Give back</u>:** At the end of the day, remember where you started, why you started and how you want to thank those who have helped you along the way. I did this by creating a firm initiative just shortly after inception. This initiative means so much to me and I'm proud that the heart of our firm is giving back to one another and our local community. I created the **One% to Give** initiative as a commitment to give back 1% of all our sales to a local organization every quarter which the firm votes on. Our agents can present

organizations near and dear to them and we also have a web form for local organizations to submit for our consideration. Paying it forward and giving back can impact all aspects of your life in ways you never thought possible—not only monetarily, but through your time and service. The highest performers are most often big givers.

My Satisfaction

I have been able to design a life that I absolutely love, and it took many years of hustle and determination to get there. More business does not always translate to being a stressed-out workaholic. In the past few years, I have more business than I ever had, and I leverage others to maintain a balance to keep my business running while freeing up my time to either generate more business or spend more time with family and friends. I encourage you to adjust to a growth mindset and be intentional and thoughtful in every part of your business if you are not already.

What is holding you back to dream big?

You only live once!

About Kristen

Kristen Haynes is a true Entrepreneur with over ten years of real estate experience and a six-figure agent after her first year selling residential real estate in 2013. After being a top producing agent for years with an independent local brokerage, she started her own firm – Triad's Finest Real Estate by eXp Realty in January 2021, where she now leads 20 agents and 6 staff members.

Kristen is an agent known for her responsiveness, keen market insight, 'bulldog' tenacity, and she is also a licensed General Contractor! This work ethic has ultimately led her to build an almost 100% referral-based business, earning Choice awards for Favorite Realtor by a local publication many years in a row. She also won the Business Journal 2023 Outstanding Women in Business award and consistently appears as one of the top agents in the Triad. As a certified luxury home marketing specialist, a Guild Member of the Institute of Luxury Home Marketing, and member of eXp Luxury division, Kristen has an additional level of understanding of what it takes to market, sell, negotiate, and purchase high-end properties. Kristen believes in giving every buyer or seller the same quality luxury experience. She's also constantly investing in her own real estate and has a portfolio of long-term and vacation rentals, residential and commercial.

Kristen graduated from North Carolina State University in 2006 and was chosen for the Leadership Development Program at BB&T where she spent the next six years. She attributes a lot of her success in real estate to the background, fundamentals and values she learned in banking. With the bank, she initially served as project manager developing sales and marketing tools before moving into commercial real estate and Corporate areas. She gained excellent communication skills and contacts while managing a portfolio of nearly $1 billion in loan exposure (not to mention skills in juggling deadlines, renewals and other client expectations).

She and her husband Jimmy, a real estate attorney, have three girls, Alice, Olivia, and Hadley. They enjoy playing tennis, golf, skiing, fishing, cooking, and spending time on Bald Head Island, in Boone, NC, and Aspen, CO.

CHAPTER 15

THE RICHES ARE IN THE NICHES

BY BETH P. SILVERMAN

What if I told you the key to earning big money in real estate was to stop looking for clients?

Stop looking for Buyers! Stop looking for Sellers! Stop looking for leads!

You'd probably tell me I'm crazy. Don't worry, I've been called worse.

You might even flip back through this book to make sure you read it correctly.

Dial. Set appointments. Dial. Go after FSBOs. Dial. Show houses. Dial. Nurture leads. Dial. Run appointments. Close. Use Social Media. Become the community Mayor. Scale. Get other people to dial.

Sound about right?

"How long does it take to earn six figures (and beyond) using that method?"

Don't ask me. I don't major in the minors.

Let me ask you this:

"Have you ever had to go to a specialist in your life, or know someone who has?"

You go to your primary care physician and something's off. They give you a diagnosis and refer you to see a specialist. You search the Internet, ask friends and Facebook for recommendations. You sit on hold with the specialist's receptionist for what seems like an eternity, only to be told the first available appointment is three weeks away, and before you can even book the appointment, they want your insurance information, and they're crystal clear you'll be responsible for whatever your insurance doesn't cover at the time of the visit? You book the appointment. After all, the problem isn't 'gonna' solve itself.

Three weeks later you see the specialist. They provide a fascinating depth of knowledge and keen insight as to what the problem is and its root cause. They offer a compelling solution to the problem and the outcome you can expect to achieve from following their prescribed course of action. The specialist becomes your trusted, go-to advisor for an extended period of time, and in some cases, you will see them regularly for a lifetime.

SPECIALISTS MAKE SPECIAL MONEY

- Specialists are always in demand because they possess a unique skill set that others do not. People seek them out for their expertise.
- If you become a specialist in a real estate niche, you won't spend your time searching for people; you'll be searching for opportunities instead. I'm 'gonna' let you in on a little secret. If you find the opportunity, the people will follow.

Noteworthy to mention, <u>the people have the money</u>.

Niches in residential real estate are all around us; community specialists such as 55+, equestrian, boating, or fly-in communities, condos, new construction, divorce real estate, REO/foreclosures, end of life/estate planning, vacant land, and my obsession, income properties. You might choose a niche based on the market you live in or having had personal experience in the space.

For me, choosing to dominate a niche meant dedicating myself to learning everything I could about becoming a residential investment specialist. It took several years to really figure it out, and my hope is that in just a few short pages you will be light years ahead of me. This space is wide open and yours for the taking, **IF**...you commit to putting in the work to master understanding the opportunities you are looking for and how to present them.

Investment Specialists are designed to withstand any and all market conditions because there is always a demand for the service they provide.

- Investors are always buying.
- They are buying and holding, buying and flipping, buying and leveraging.

But why?

Quite simply, to build wealth, people need to diversify their money and put it to work for them. Depositing money in the bank doesn't do much of anything in terms of short and long term growth (the stock market and crypto can be volatile and downright unnerving at times), but the housing market. The housing market is far more predictable in terms of short term gains and long term appreciation.

We've weathered recessions, crashes, lumber and labor shortages, a pandemic, inflation, and guess what? Through all of those cycles one thing never changes. People need shelter.

And we're a couple million homes short of meeting the existing demand. If the demand far outweighs the supply, you can imagine working with Real Estate investors is a very rewarding venture for everyone.

When done properly, **the average investor buys two or more doors per year.**

- The lifetime value of an investor versus the lifetime value of a traditional buyer or seller is nearly 10X. Take that in for a moment.
- What if you didn't need a huge sphere or database?
- What if you built a pod of about twenty investors who transacted fifty times a year with you? Would that make for a lucrative career as a solo agent?

Unfortunately, I can't show you my bank accounts of years past, but I can tell you I've been broke, I had more debt than imaginable from student loans and getting cancer in my late twenties, my FICO score was in the 500's, I needed credit cards to survive, and when I moved to Florida six years ago I knew one person and one neighborhood. **How was I going to make it as a Realtor when I didn't even know anyone?** No one was looking for me.

Never one to quit in the face of fear and uncertainty, I decided if people weren't going to look for me I needed to bring the opportunity to them.

But what was the opportunity and who were the people I needed to bring it to?

First I had to answer two key questions:

(1). Who is a Real Estate investor? ...and
(2). What types of investment properties are there?

(1). Who is a Real Estate Investor?

A Real Estate Investor is anyone who desires to build wealth by using the housing market as the vehicle. The key word in that sentence is **anyone**. Anyone who desires short term gains and long term appreciation, anyone who wants to earn passive income by strategically purchasing real estate, is a real estate investor.

You've probably done a few rental transactions in your career, stored those clients in your CRM, engaged in conversation about becoming a first time home buyer. Maybe you set them up with your trusted lending partner, invited them to a first time buyer seminar, got them credit counseling, and prayed to the real estate gods they'd be ready to buy a house in your local market in 12-15 months.

This is so much more fun than that!

For starters, you're not just looking for people in your local market. Savvy real estate investors know the best deals are not in their backyard. The people you bring the opportunity to don't come from farming or door knocking one zip code, they come from all over the globe. The power of video and the reach of social media is so vast that if you have the right opportunity, the investors will come to you.

Don't believe me?

That broke girl, riddled with debt, who doubted if she could survive without going back to a corporate sales job, who came to Florida six years ago on a hope and a prayer to build a real estate business without knowing anyone, is now debt free, with an 820 FICO score, a fancy car in the garage, a growing real estate portfolio, new clients who wait one to two weeks to get on my schedule, who don't get to me without going through a financial vetting process, who pay an additional fee to work with me and have access to my trusted vendor partners, who continue to transact multiple times a year and refer business to me, without ever having to buy a lead or send a mailer. This is the life I built. And you can, too.

Specialists make special money but all of this is moot without the opportunity.

(2). What types of residential investment properties are there?

o **Long Term Rental** (LTR): dwellings leased for one month or longer. These properties can be unfurnished or furnished. They can be rented monthly (if permissible by zoning regulations), seasonally, or annually to a tenant with renewable or non-renewable terms at lease end.

o **Co-living**: Similar to a long term rental, but these leases are by the room instead of an entire dwelling. Utilities are often included in the rent.

o **Short Term Rental** (STR): Furnished dwellings rented under 30 days, vacation rentals such as Airbnb, or corporate rentals. Depending upon zoning and county ordinances, these properties can be rented for one night, several days, one week, two weeks, etc.

o **Multi-Family**: a Dwelling containing more than one unit, such as a duplex, triplex, or quadplex (anything 5 or more is commercial, which carries commercial loan products, commercial interest rates, and commercial insurance). These dwellings are zoned multi-family with separate meters, and can be attached by walls, or detached from one another.

o **Fix and Flip: Buy, Rehab, Sell**.

o **Accessory Dwelling Unit** (ADU): A secondary house or apartment that shares the same lot and cannot be sold separately. Can be attached or detached. Sometimes referred to as an in-law suite, guest house, carriage house, garage apartment. ADU's are viewed as an extension of the main dwelling and are not separately metered. Utilities are usually included in the lease.

There are pros and cons to investing in each of these properties and depending on the goals and finances of the investor and current market trends, one might be a better choice than another.

You'll need to familiarize yourself with this information:

Google and YouTube are your free best friends; use them before you waste thousands on some random online course.

While you're there, learn the following terms and definitions: BRRR, Cap rate, vacancy rate, net operating income, cash flow, cash on cash return, proforma, hard money, 1031 exchange, HELOC, cash out re-fi.

Practice analyzing a long term rental property first. This is often the gateway to all other investments, and if you're fairly new and don't have a handle on market trends and housing statistics, analyzing flips and short term rentals takes a lot more practice. The MLS is your bible. Every day should start and end there. Real Estate investing is about dollars and sense. Find the opportunities that make sense.

Is this starting to sound hard, like it's too much to learn?

Are you thinking this isn't for you?

Look, maybe you enjoy talking to sellers about painting the walls 'Agreeable Gray' before they list, and maybe you love showing an emotional buyer 46 homes before finally getting them under contract. If that's the case, go be the best at it!

My real estate coach, Micheal Burt, always says, "I'm looking for Navy Seals not baby seals." Gets me every time. Specialists require special education.

You get paid the big bucks when you possess a unique skill set that others do not.

I believe I can help anyone generate passive income, build long term wealth, and achieve financial freedom through strategic real estate investing.

I believe I can show any Realtor who is hungry, humble, and coachable, how to succeed in this space.

So how do we go from idea to action?

There are three things an investment specialist must excel in:

1) **Procuring Properties** – The MLS is your bible.
2) **Analyzing Properties** – A calculator, google mortgage calculator, and a proforma will get you going.
3) **Pitching Properties** – You found the opportunity! Now tell the people what you have (without giving away the location or all the details until you collect their info and qualify them). Use social media to reach a global audience.

And for an added bonus:

Positioning the Property After the Sale – This will ensure you over-deliver and set your investor up for success. If you can master showing investors how to best position their properties (with the help of your trusted vendor tribe), they will be exceedingly loyal, they will transact with you frequently, refer an abundance of business to you, and you will grow and build wealth together.

When I look back at how many people I've helped generate passive income and build generational wealth it's astonishing. From all walks of life, all with different reasons, different goals, different financials, who share the same vision to use real estate as the vehicle to lead them to where they want to go, faster. I'm amazed by the diverse community of investors and vendors I've built. And what's wild is the opportunities continue to grow more abundant every year, so much so that I need to remind myself to stop and look at what I've built.

There will never again come a time where I worry about being broke. There will never again come a time where I live deal to deal, paycheck to paycheck, have to rely on a credit card to buy anything, or question whether or not I chose the right career.

There is safety in this niche. A shift cannot break your business. An economic downturn cannot break your business. There is always a season to invest in real estate. Never wait for an investor to come to you. Bring the opportunity to the investor. The better you become at finding opportunities that make you stand out in this niche, the more you will illuminate a bright light on your talent and establish yourself as a trusted advisor. Do this, and people will come in droves.

Now go and get yourself a few stacks of that special money.

About Beth

Beth P. Silverman is an Investment Specialist / Mentor / ICON agent.

Everything starts and ends with the belief that anyone can achieve financial freedom and generate passive income through strategic Real Estate Investments. For the investors and Realtors who partner with Beth Silverman as their expert advisor, the sky is not the limit, but merely the beginning.

A native of Long Island, New York, Beth got her start in Real Estate working for a developer in new construction in 2008. In 2010, she returned to Baltimore, Maryland, (Johns Hopkins Alum) and began her career as an REO agent working heavily in the fix and flip space. Beth quickly mastered finding off-market opportunities, analyzing returns and how to utilize investment strategies such as a 1031 exchange to help clients generate wealth quickly.

In 2018, Beth moved the business to the pristine gulf beaches of Saint Petersburg, Florida, and became heavily immersed in short term vacation rentals (STRs). She assembled a tribe of vendors who played a critical role in the acquisition and sale of over 70 high-performing beach STRs in under five years.

Beth became a leading Realtor Partner of the co-living platform, Padsplit, where she helps investors generate 2 to 3X more monthly revenue on rental properties and brings awareness for the need for affordable workforce housing throughout the nation.

Understanding Market trends, the economy, and where the housing market is headed, combined with her explosive energy, dynamic stage presence, and obsession with helping people generate passive income, have been key factors in what sets Beth apart from the competition.

Teaching Realtors how to succeed in the niche real estate space is something Beth is extraordinarily passionate about. She was named eXp Realty's 2022 Instructor of the Year. Beth is a two time ICON agent who believes with the right guidance and support monumental success is always within reach.

When Beth is not busy with her real estate obsession, you can find her enjoying a cigar and soaking up the sun in and around St Pete.

Connect with Beth:

- https://www.instagram.com/floridamoveswithbeth/